D1270447

NESS/SCIENCE/TECHNOLOGY DIVISION
CHICAGO PUBLIC LIBRARY
400 SOUTH STATE STREET
CHICAGO, IL 60605

REVOLT ON GOOSE ISLAND

THE CHICAGO FACTORY TAKEOVER, AND
WHAT IT SAYS ABOUT THE ECONOMIC CRISIS

REVOLT ON GOOSE ISLAND

THE CHICAGO FACTORY TAKEOVER, AND WHAT IT SAYS ABOUT THE ECONOMIC CRISIS

KARI LYDERSEN

MELVILLEHOUSE
BROOKLYN, NEW YORK

R0422657924

THE CHICAGO PUBLIC LIBRARY

Dedicated to Franklin Rosemont (1943-2009)
Author, poet, publisher, activist, surrealist and idealist who
chronicled the labor movement with creativity and joy.

© Kari Lydersen, 2009

Melville House Publishing
145 Plymouth Street
Brooklyn, New York 11201

www.mhpbooks.com

First Melville House Printing: June 2009

Book Design: Kelly Blair

Library of Congress Cataloging-in-Publication Data

Lydersen, Kari.
 Revolt on Goose Island / Kari Lydersen.
    p. cm.
 ISBN 978-1-933633-82-4
 1. Sit-down strikes--Illinois--Chicago. I. Title.
 HD5474.L94 2009
 331.892'8901820977311--dc22

                              2009016787

CONTENTS

11 Preface

15 The Stakeout

37 A Labor Battle in a Labor City

57 Shutting the Door on Republic

69 The Revolt

101 A Window of Opportunity

111 Getting Serious

127 On the Road to Resistance and Recovery

157 Epilogue

163 Notes

UE union Local 1110 President Armando Robles addresses the media about negotiations with Bank of America and Republic Windows & Doors on the fourth day of the sit-in at the factory. (AP Photo/M. Spencer Green)

PREFACE

In early December 2008, headlines around the world focused on the workers of the Republic Windows & Doors factory in Chicago, Illinois. There, 250 workers had been laid off after the abrupt shut-down of their factory. The closing wasn't unusual—it came in the midst of the largest economic collapse since the Great Depression, at a moment when every day brought news of more job losses. Just days before the closing, the U.S. Labor Department announced more than a half million job cuts.

But the company's workers did something unusual.

Represented by the UE labor union, they occupied the fac-tory, located on Goose Island in the Chicago River, and refused to leave until they were paid for accrued vacation time and 60 days of federally-mandated severance.

Congressmen, local politicians and President-Elect Barack Obama spoke out in support of the workers. Soon-to-be-impeached Governor Rod Blagojevich even made his last public appearance at the factory before being arrested on massive corruption charges.

Republic owner Richard Gillman blamed Bank of America for the closing, saying the bank had cut off credit to the company. The truth proved to be more complicated, but blaming the bank struck a chord with Americans fed up with corporate greed and skeptical of the $700 billion federal bank bailout, which members of Congress and the sitting administration had promised would unfreeze the credit markets. Bank of America had received $25 billion in bailout funds two months before Republic closed; it would receive another $20 billion soon after. "You got bailed out, we got sold out!" became a rallying cry for people around the country protesting in support of the Republic workers and against the bank.

The workers' story captured the imagination and empathy of a nation cast caught in an escalating economic crisis. People who had felt secure in their jobs and firmly ensconced in the middle class were suddenly finding themselves out of work or terrified of becoming so. And so, many eyes turned to the tactics being used at Republic. According to Reverend Jesse Jackson, the takeover represented "the beginning of a larger movement for mass action to resist economic violence."

In Republic's case, the workers' tactics were successful. Pressure was applied to America's largest financial institutions—Bank of America and JPMorgan Chase—and a settlement was eventually reached with the workers. What's more, there was also another significant victory, one that held out the possibility of reopening the Republic plant. These new developments were in some ways lost in the country's ongoing economic woes. There was also a string of significant events in Chicago that obscured the evolving situation at Republic—from the Obama transition to the ousting and later impeachment of Illinois Governor Rod Blagojevich.

Many union organizers, labor experts and citizens heralded the Republic victories as potential harbingers of a revitalized and reinvigorated labor movement in the U.S. Those involved point out that far from being a spontaneous act, it was the result of finely-tuned and tireless organizing and strategizing, by an independent union that has forged a path separate from most organized labor and with a workforce largely comprised of Latino immigrants. The Republic story thus entwines some of the most significant questions facing the U.S. economy: the evolving situation of organized labor; the increasing role of immigrants in the economy; the potential impact of the bank bailouts; as well as a significant connection to the economic "stimulus" package passed in February 2009.

If any lasting impact is to come from the Republic victory, workers and supporters say, their story will have to be kept alive. This book offers a deeper look into the events and underlying forces leading up to, during and after the revolt on Goose Island.

© David Schalliol

CHAPTER ONE

THE STAKEOUT

"Turn out all the lights right now," a supervisor at Republic Windows & Doors told Armando Robles as he was wrapping up the second shift at the factory on Goose Island, a small hive of industry sitting in the middle of the Chicago River. It was about 10 p.m. on November 5, 2008. Robles thought the order strange, as other employees were still finishing up. "Everyone has to leave right now," the supervisor said. For a while Robles and other workers had been suspicious about the health of the company and strange occurrences at the factory. They knew business had been bad for the past two years. The housing crash meant not many people were in the market for new windows and doors, neither Republic's higher-end ornate grooved, wood-framed glass panes nor their utilitarian vinyl- and aluminum-framed windows. At monthly "town hall meetings" that the company had started holding over the past year, managers were constantly bemoaning how much money they were losing. And the workforce had been nearly cut in half in the past few years, from about 500 to 250. Something seemed to be up, and Robles felt sure it wasn't good.

He alerted fellow worker Sergio Revuelta, a union steward with eight years at the company. The two left the building as if nothing was amiss, then huddled outside the plant. They watched as the plant manager and a former manager came out and looked around carefully. Five cars drove up. That was strange. "It was all faces and cars we recognized, former employees and former supervisors," said Revuelta later. Robles and Revuelta watched as the men began removing boxes and pieces of machinery from the low-slung, inconspicuous warehouse. They crept around to the back, where they saw a U-Haul truck waiting with its lights off. Over the next few hours, they watched a parade of objects being loaded into the truck. They were shivering by this time, as they had been sitting in Revuelta's car, and he had sold the car's ailing heater to a junkyard. The only illumination came from the light on a forklift. They stayed all night; it wasn't until almost 5 a.m. that they finally headed home to their families. "We knew something was going to happen, we wanted to watch and see if we were right," remembered Revuelta, 36. "When we saw the stuff coming out, I said, 'Bingo!'"

Revuelta was among the many workers who suspected that Republic management was trying to move their operation elsewhere and deprive them of their jobs. It was a highly disturbing thought.

Most of the Republic employees had been there for 10 years or more. The most senior employee had 34 years at the plant. And almost three-quarters of them had come to the United States from Mexico, leaving families and homes behind. Some might have paid thousands of dollars to "coyotes" to lead them across the border, may have walked for days through the stifling heat of the desert, trudging through a seemingly endless landscape of barren, rocky hills and deep arroyos where feet sunk into the soft crumbly dirt. Thousands of Mexicans every year spend this money and take this risk—an average of more than one person per day dies crossing the border—in hopes of getting jobs like those at Republic, earning decent enough wages to bring their families to the United States and also send money to relatives back in Mexico. Many immigrants work at temporary jobs, waiting on streetcorners on blazing summer days or in the freezing winter to be picked up for construction or transient factory work. Those who land steady union jobs like the ones at Republic, with health benefits and paid vacations, would not give them up easily.

The news of the suspicious night quickly spread to other workers. Robles' friend Melvin "Ricky" Maclin later heard a similar story from a distraught secretary who said most of the office furniture had been removed. "There was nowhere for them to sit, all the tables, chairs, computers, and file cabinets were gone," remembers Maclin. He laughed at the bizarre predicament described by the office worker faced with an empty office, but the woman told him it wasn't funny. The atmosphere had become so tense and strange at the factory that the clerical staff were afraid to speak up, and as they weren't in the union like the shop-floor workers, they felt they had no one to speak up for them. In the following days, Robles and other workers were ordered to load heavy machinery from the factory onto semi-truck trailers. Sometimes, they were first told to replace components on the machinery with new ones. They saw deliveries being unloaded at Republic that weren't intended for their plant. One time, a brand-new and mysterious piece of machinery was dropped off after a plant engineer's mother said it could not be stored in her garage, Robles remembers. The workers knew this equipment wasn't going to be used at Republic, so what was the company up to?

When they asked managers what was going on, they got vague answers about the machinery being sold to raise money or being sent away for repairs. On Monday, November 17, a whole team of workers who normally made the "Allure" line of windows arrived with no jobs to do, since the machines they usually worked on were gone. Union representatives started filing written requests for information; under their collective bargaining agreement with the company, the union had the right to be advised of major operating decisions or changes. The workers were represented by Local 1110 of the United Electrical Radio and Machine Workers of America, or UE, a scrappy, progressive union with a storied activist history. But they got no response. Workers got more and more suspicious and angry.

"I asked my supervisor, 'How can I work when I don't even know if you can pay me?'" said Rocio Perez, a single mother of five and union steward. She felt like the managers viewed them as gullible and naïve since they expected them to keep working as the factory was obviously being dismantled under their noses. "It was like they were mocking us."

The workers organized a surveillance team that would keep watch outside the factory after hours and on weekends, when the plant was closed. One Saturday, Robles and Revuelta were lurking in the parking lot north of the factory, Robles with his wife Patricia and their young son Oscar in tow. They could see the plant's front entrance on Hickory Street, where boxes were being loaded onto two trailer trucks. They hopped into their cars: Revuelta drove out after the first trailer, and Robles followed the second one. He wasn't frightened or intimidated, only determined to see what the company was up to. The union's contract covers any activity within a 40-mile radius of the plant, and rumors were circulating that the equipment was being moved to Joliet, an industrial town exactly 40 miles outside Chicago.

The two men took note of the trucks' license plates and followed them for about 15 miles to a truckyard on the southwest side of the city, an industrial, grimy swath of land next to the highway. They parked just outside the yard and, keeping their eyes on the now-stationary trailers, Robles called international union representative Mark Meinster, a 35-year-old Philadelphia native who had been an activist since high school. After studying history at a small college in Pennsylvania, Meinster worked for the national community organizing group ACORN in Washington D.C. But he became convinced organized labor was the best realm to press for larger social change, and in 2002 he moved to Chicago to work for the UE as an international rep, responsible for collective bargaining and worker education in Illinois and Wisconsin.

Meinster asked Robles if they could hold tight for an hour. Robles wasn't planning to go anywhere. By the time Meinster arrived it was getting dark and cold. They sat inside the car for almost four hours mulling over what they should do. Robles was mad. He has a bright smile and is quick to laugh, but when he senses injustice or unfairness he is equally quick to anger and has no qualms about speaking his mind. That's one of the reasons his co-workers had voted him president of the union local a year and a half earlier.

"I have a friend who drives trailer trucks. We could steal the trailers, then they would have to negotiate with us," Robles suggested to Meinster. "Or we could deflate the tires." The union rep appreciated Robles' fearlessness but talked him out of his schemes. They hit upon another idea, one with a long and glorious history in union lore: they could occupy the plant. Robles immediately liked the idea. In other countries, including his native Mexico, factory occupations are fairly common. But in the United States the tactic had not been used other than in a few scattered cases since organized labor's heyday in the 1930s, when auto workers brought the industry's top companies to their knees with sit-down strikes. Occupying the factory would likely mean that people would be arrested, Robles realized, and there was no guarantee it would work or even gain popular support. But these were economic times unlike any in the past 30 years, and drastic times call for drastic measures.

Over the following days, Meinster and Robles bounced the occupation idea off other workers, and they quickly found six people ready and willing to risk arrest and occupy the plant in the case of a closing or mass layoff. Some workers were not citizens, on probation for minor criminal offenses, or had no one to take care of their children, so they couldn't risk it. But most everyone who heard about the idea was enthusiastic and vowed to be outside picketing if a takeover started. "I said, 'Let's do it!' We had to do something to get some respect," said Revuelta. "We don't know why some bosses just treat the workers like nothing, but we can't let them do that."

Meinster was aware the Canadian Auto Workers union had in recent years undertaken several dramatic factory occupations or blockades. In July 2008, an auto parts factory near Toronto closed abruptly; workers only learned about the shutdown from news reports, and they received no severance pay. "We were just thrown out on the street to go straight to the garbage bin," a machine operator told the media.[1] The company, Progressive Moulded Products, had closed a dozen plants, axing more than 2,000 jobs. Workers blockaded the entrances, preventing Ford, Chrysler, and GM from removing equipment, as the auto giants had been doing at a number of recently shuttered Canadian parts plants. As in the United States, the workers would have been last in line for pay as the company went into bankruptcy. Though these workers were non-union, the Canadian Auto Workers (CAW) supported their blockade. The previous year, union Canadian auto workers had occupied a parts plant that had closed in Scarborough and prevented the removal of equipment. That occupation ended victoriously, as the major U.S. automakers who bought their parts from the company put up several million dollars for the severance pay mandated in the Canadian workers' contracts.[2]

Meinster had never undertaken anything like this before, so he began to do his homework. He made a few calls to his Canadian counterparts to visualize the nuts and bolts of occupying a factory.

This included logistics—how to get food into the plant, how to bail people out in case of arrests—and strategy. What would their demands be? Who would be their target?

Over the next few weeks, the workers kept making windows and doors at the factory, but the uncertainty and tensions heightened each day. Plant operations manager Tim Widner told workers he was quitting to become a fifth grade teacher in Ohio. Workers didn't buy it for a second; they figured he must be going to the same place as all their machinery. "When he said that was when we really knew they were lying through their teeth," said Meinster. The situation was obviously coming to a head. Over Thanksgiving weekend, the plant would be closed for four days. The union organized four-hour surveillance shifts to run around the clock. Most of the workers were looking forward to big family get-togethers over the holidays, but the situation at the factory cast a pall over everything. It's hard to look forward to Christmas when you're afraid you won't have a job.

A FACTORY ON AN ISLAND

In 1965, William Spielman formed Republic Windows & Doors, a small family business on the southwest side of Chicago making low-cost storm windows and doors. Spielman's business grew quickly, and he moved it to a larger location in Lincoln Park on the north side of the city, which was then a hardscrabble neighborhood home to many working-class Puerto Rican residents and with a smattering of heavy industry. Spielman's nephew Richard

Gillman started working as a salesman for the company in 1974.[3] During the 1980s, the business expanded by leaps and bounds. For its first two decades the company had largely targeted home-improvement contractors, selling them relatively small orders of windows and doors specifically tailored to their residential projects. Many of these contractors were small, often family-run operations. Then, in the mid '80s, Republic began producing vinyl replacement windows and patio doors, expanding their market to include businesses, factories, and large apartment complexes and subdivisions across the region.[4]

When William Spielman died his son Ron took over the business. In the mid-1990s, Republic moved to a new location, in an inconspicuous but sprawling warehouse-type building that the company purchased a few miles away on Goose Island.

Goose Island is the Chicago River's only island, a 160-acre chunk formed in 1853 by the building of a canal. Irish immigrants who moved onto the island coined its name. They raised livestock, farmed, and worked in small factories. Soon Polish and German immigrants joined them in worker housing built on the island. No bridge connected it to the mainland until after the Chicago Fire of 1871. By the late 1800s, the island was packed with heavy industry, including two grain elevators, 11 coal yards, many leather tanneries, various other factories . . . and plenty of taverns. Chicago at this time was a commercial and industrial hub for the whole country, thanks to its position on Lake Michigan and at the crux of rail lines, and Goose Island was right in the heart of it all. It was called "Little Hell" for the billowing smoke and soot, and people began to move away from the island. Over time, so did much of the industry.[5] But history-obsessed Chicagoans remained fond of the island; the Goose Island brewpub located just north of the island spread its name to beer lovers around the country. In the 1980s, as professionals who had fled the city for the suburbs gravitated back to newly trendy lofts and apartments downtown, there was a debate over Goose Island's future. Some developers envisioned it hosting prime luxury riverfront housing, even though the sluggish river was still relatively polluted. But Mayor Richard M. Daley and other politicians wanted Goose Island to return to its industrial roots, and Daley instituted a plan in 1990 to further this goal, giving subsidies to industry and making it illegal within a certain zone to turn factories into housing.[6] Hence Republic and its neighboring factories were part of a larger municipal vision for revitalizing Chicago's legacy as the "city of big shoulders."

Division Street runs across Goose Island; metal bridges on either side clank and clatter as semi-trucks drive across. To the east are the Cabrini Green housing projects, now largely dismantled as part of the city's plan to redevelop the infamous, crumbling, crime-ridden, public housing high-rises into "mixed income" developments—displacing many of the public housing residents in the process. To the east of Cabrini Green, there were vacant buildings and a few liquor stores and social-service agencies; now there are new condos, a beautifully manicured park, a Starbucks, and other chain stores. To the west of Goose Island is a small swath of industry, including the blazing furnaces of the Finkl & Sons steel mill, and the trendy, gentrifying neighborhood of Wicker Park. Goose Island itself is now home to various light manufacturing facilities and warehouses. One of Republic's neighbors, the Five Star Hotel Laundry, was the site of another drawn-out, high-profile, and highly contentious labor struggle led by immigrants: in 2000, Latinas won the right to be represented by the UNITE union after a citywide campaign that included pickets at downtown hotels. At the northern tip of Goose Island, like the helm of a ship, sits the William Wrigley, Jr. Co.'s Global Innovation Center, a modern glass structure where the century-old company tests new gum and candy products and flavors.[7] In 2005, the same year in which the Innovation Center opened, Wrigley closed its last Chicago gum factory, laying off 600 workers.[8]

In 1996, the city committed almost $10 million to help Republic establish the new site and to grow. The money came out of tax increment financing (TIF) funds, a controversial program wherein an area is designated as "blighted" and then property taxes are diverted to fund development meant to revitalize the neighborhood. The diversion of property-tax dollars means less money for schools and parks. And in Chicago, some of the city's toniest neighborhoods have been designated "blighted" TIF zones. Critics describe the program as a way for city officials to give handouts to favored developers. Republic's TIF funding came with the stipulation that the factory maintain 549 jobs for at least eight years and make "reasonable commercial efforts" to maintain more than 600 jobs until 2019.[9]

The new Goose Island facility was spacious, sterile, and state-of-the-art, with the latest in machinery, comfortable cafeterias and break rooms, even a gym. A building contractor who was a long-time customer was impressed during a tour of the factory. But he thought the company was in over its head. He said the quality of their products had declined after the move and he stopped buying from Republic in 2000. He felt that the needs of small contractors like himself were no longer a priority for the company, saying, "They wanted to sell semi-truck loads, not pickup-truck loads" to developers of subdivisions all over the Midwest.[10]

Under Ron Spielman's watch, Republic had skyrocketed from a modest local supplier to a regional industry powerhouse. But the success was not to last long. People familiar with the company, including union officials, workers, and the aforementioned building contractor, thought it was being poorly managed, or perhaps intentionally run in a way not conducive to long term survival. "They were highly respected in the industry, but whether it was bad business decisions or corruption they certainly didn't do what they needed to keep the business going well," said UE organizer Mark Meinster.

In May 2004 Republic began supplying windows to Pacesetter, an Omaha-based home improvement company that had recently closed its own window factory, laying off 70 union members. It was a multi-million dollar contract and could have been a boon for Republic. But Pacesetter was suffering severe financial troubles of its own, resulting partly from changes in federal law that hampered its once-thriving telemarketing sales. Pacesetter quickly fell behind in payments to Republic. Republic kept delivering windows even though they weren't getting paid, since they figured cutting off deliveries would drive Pacesetter further into decline and make it even less likely Republic would eventually be paid.

But by summer 2005 Republic cut off sales to Pacesetter, and later that year Pacesetter began bankruptcy proceedings. Republic lost $4 million in the debacle, which prompted Spielman to step aside and turn the company over to his cousin, Richard Gillman.[11] Gillman took majority ownership without paying a penny but rather by assuming a debt load of about $30 million.[12] Around this time, Republic also sold its building to the Wrigley company, which leased it back to Republic. That cash influx helped, and Gillman got to work looking for new investments. He hired a bright young businessman named Barry Dubin to be the company's new chief operating officer.

Dubin, a Chicago native with a mop of curly hair and a friendly grin, graduated from St. Ignatius, one of the city's top prep schools, in 1995 and studied business at Indiana University and at the prestigious Kellogg School of Management at Northwestern University.[13]

In early 2007, Dubin recruited JPMorgan Chase & Co. to take a 40-percent equity stake in the company as a flagship of its newly launched Chase Capital investment program for "alternative capital solutions to middle market companies." Chase Capital co-head Dave Schabes said in a press release that they chose Republic because "it has worked very hard over the past 15 months to reduce its costs and improve its quality, timeliness, and productivity. We are confident that the company can continue to build on this significant progress."[14]

"We had been searching for an investor that believed in Republic's potential for growth and valued our longstanding reputation as an innovator in the building products industry," said Dubin in a press release issued by Republic. "We found that partner in Chase Capital."

Dubin was promised a $60,000 bonus to be paid later, for his role in the Chase deal, and he and Gillman celebrated along with about eight other staff members with a retreat—billed to the company—at the luxurious Bellagio Hotel in Las Vegas.[15]

In January 2007, Gillman also got a $5 million line of secured credit from Bank of America. Such a credit line is based on formulas determining the borrower's ability to repay, and it is backed by collateral and assets that will essentially revert to the lender if the borrower defaults. Though it was initiated as a $5 million line, with such a loan that amount would be constantly reevaluated depending on the borrower's financial health. So if the business went downhill, its available credit could be reduced.[16]

This new investment seemed to mean a new beginning for the company. But any optimism about Republic's prospects soon turned out to be misplaced. In the summer of 2007, a mortgage crisis began to mushroom out of control, quickly infecting the whole housing market and the rest of the economy. Federal Reserve chairman Ben Bernanke had said the crisis would be "contained," and government and banking officials tried to reassure the American public. But the downward spiral continued. The widespread practice of banks bundling mortgage-backed securities and selling them off to investors had exploded like a balloon. People defaulted on their mortgages, many of them sub-prime or fraudulently orchestrated mortgages that the buyers could never really afford in the first place, and went into foreclosure. As it became clear that the mortgages would not be paid, the mortgage-backed securities plummeted in value and the house of cards began to fall. Banks panicked and clamped down on offering new credit, which of course put a big chill on consumer spending, housing rehabs, and construction, new businesses, and, in a domino effect, almost every market sector.

New home-buying ground to a near standstill, even as housing prices dropped precipitously. Relatively few people now had the funds, confidence, or available credit to purchase new homes. And foreclosures were putting a significant chunk of housing back on the market, at bargain-basement prices, meaning that there was even less demand for new housing. If new houses, office buildings, and condos were not being built, new windows and doors were not being purchased to put in them. There was still some window and door demand for rehabs and repairs, but this market also slowed as families and developers put off plans for upgrades and delayed all but the most crucial repairs.[17]

In this climate, it didn't take long for Republic to burn through its $5 million line of credit, according to Bank of America Midwest government relations manager Pat Holden. The company lost the equivalent of the credit line, about $5 million, in 2007.[18] In February 2008, Bank of America officials told Gillman that they were concerned about his company's situation and advised him to find new investors and lenders or consider shutting the business down.[19]

By July 2008, the company's financial situation didn't look any better; Republic had lost about $3.6 million in just six months. Bank of America officials told Gillman that if he didn't get another lender he should "start winding down operations"; in other words, get ready to close the company and presumably sell off the assets to pay back the bank and other creditors. Holden said Gillman ignored their advice and continued asking for more credit. The bank said no. It isn't clear if Gillman was making any payments on his loan or how much he was asking from Bank of America— Holden said such information was confidential. Bankruptcy documents filed later indicate that by the time the company shut down, it owed the bank more than $6 million.[20]

Holden emphasized that Republic's woes went beyond the expected effects of the housing crisis followed by the larger economic crisis. It was simply a badly run company, in the view of bank officials, and financial troubles that had plagued it for years were only exacerbated by the housing collapse. Given the fact that Republic had lost almost $10 million in less than two years as of the summer of 2008, Holden said there was no way the bank could continue to give them credit.

"The company had simply used it up and there was no more left for them to borrow," said Holden. "They were bleeding, they were hemorrhaging. We could not extend an additional loan to them. It wouldn't be prudent since it would probably not be paid back."

A BIG BANK

The company now known as Bank of America started as the Massachusetts Bank in 1784, five years before George Washington became the nation's first president. John Hancock signed the bank's original charter. It was the second bank to receive a state charter and one of only three commercial banks in the country at the time.

"Generation after generation, the financial institutions that are part of the Bank of America legacy have played a role in the development of our nation's culture and economy," says the bank's website proudly.[21]

A lot has changed in the 225 years since the founding of the bank's predecessor. Now it is a trillion-dollar-plus institution with operations throughout the United States, Europe, Asia, the Middle East, and Latin America. In the United States it has about 6,000 bank offices serving more than 50 million customers. Its global investments cover sectors including oil, real estate, health care, aerospace and automotive. In 2007, the bank had $68 billion in revenue and $1.7 trillion in total assets.

But the bank's 2007 annual report called that "a disappointing year for our company." The first six months weren't so bad, but after the summer's housing crash the bank saw its fortunes "severely depressed by rising credit costs and the impact of the unprecedented turbulence in the financial markets."

Although the annual report expressed hope that this situation would improve in 2008, that turned out not to be the case. Like the rest of the country's financial institutions, Bank of America was heading down a treacherous path that would culminate in the previously unheard-of suggestion that the U.S. government should actually nationalize banks. However, even as Bank of America's own crisis escalated, it spent the time acquiring other floundering financial institutions, with aid from a federal government desperate not to see these institutions collapse. In October 2007, Bank of America acquired LaSalle Bank, making it the biggest bank in Chicago and Detroit. It had previously acquired U.S. Trust in 2007, MBNA in 2006, and Fleet Boston in 2004. In July 2008, Bank of America took over Countrywide Financial Corporation, notorious for its subprime loans, in a $4 billion transaction that made it the country's largest mortgage lender.[22] Bank of America pledged to "continue its long-established policy of not originating subprime mortgages," and noted its commitment to work on $40 billion worth of troubled mortgages to help 265,000 homeowners stay in their homes.[23]

In October 2008, Bank of America was granted $25 billion in bailout funds as part of the $700 billion federal bailout, otherwise known as TARP, or the Troubled Assets Relief Program. In coming months the program would garner much criticism from Congress and the general public for throwing money at banks while seemingly doing little to help distressed mortgage holders or loosen frozen credit markets. After a first round of bailout funds was dispersed, Bank of America, like other major recipients, was criticized for a lack of transparency in its use of the money.[24] The bank used the funds in part to acquire Merrill Lynch, the once-mighty brokerage firm then facing collapse as part of the larger Wall Street meltdown. (In January, the U.S. Treasury would grant Bank of America an additional $20 billion in TARP funds to help with the rocky Merrill Lynch takeover.)

As Bank of America was preparing for the takeover, Merrill Lynch CEO John Thain was trying to get some last-minute perks. He lobbied to be paid a multi-million-dollar bonus, even as his company was reporting $15.3 billion fourth-quarter losses. He completed a million-dollar office redecoration and took a vacation to a luxury ski resort in Vail, Colorado.[25] Thain became a timely model of the type of top-heavy and greedy businessman that many blamed for getting the country into this mess.

Meanwhile, in December 2008, Bank of America announced probable layoffs of 30,000 to 35,000 employees from its own and Merrill Lynch's workforces over the course of three years, which represented up to 11 percent of the bank's global employees. This was in addition to 11,150 people already laid off by the bank, among more than 186,000 people losing their jobs at banks since the financial crisis had started in July 2007.[26] In the first weeks of 2009, Bank of America notified the federal government of 460 layoffs in four states. Employees at the bank's Charlotte, North Carolina headquarters reported watching their colleagues lose their jobs with little warning, never knowing from day to day who would be next. One worker told *The Charlotte Observer*, "It's almost like a bomb went off and you don't know till afterward who's alive and who's dead."[27]

Many of these laid-off employees were angry about being told they were out in the cold—like the Republic workers—while the majority of CEOs (nine out of 10 according to an Associated Press investigation) who led their companies into dire financial straits were still at work earning top dollar. The Associated Press quoted a laid-off Kentucky Bank of America worker, struggling mother of three Rebecca Trevino:

> The same people at the top are still there, the same people who made the decisions causing a lot of our financial crisis. But that's what tends to happen in leadership. The people at the top, there's always some other place to lay blame. It is surprising that leadership can make decisions that lead to financial ruin for so many, and then get bailed out for it.[28]

UE representative Leah Fried with workers at the Republic factory.
(Photo © David Schalliol)

CHAPTER TWO

A LABOR BATTLE IN A LABOR CITY

Chicago is a city famous for its labor history. It was the cradle of the struggle for the eight-hour day, including the 1886 Haymarket riot that led to four anarchist labor organizers being hanged in retribution for a bomb that killed civilians and at least eight police officers at a rally. A statue commemorating the police officers killed in Haymarket was vandalized so many times that the city government eventually gave up on displaying it in public. Chicago was also home of numerous bloody and groundbreaking labor struggles through the first half of the twentieth century, among steelworkers, textile workers, railroad porters, carpenters, and others.

When Armando Robles started working at Republic, the workers were represented by a union called the Central States Joint Board (CSJB) that was well known in Chicago labor circles for ties to organized crime. Robles got the job thanks to his brother who worked there; he had tired of working the overnight shift at another factory where he had been employed for 11 years since coming to the United States from Guadalajara, Mexico. Robles didn't even know that the Republic workers had a union until a co-worker showed him how dues were deducted from his paycheck. He had never seen representatives of the union, and he was never informed of any meetings or ways he could have a say in union business. The CSJB rarely filed grievances on behalf of workers.

Then, in late 2001, it came time for the union to negotiate a new contract. Many workers were shocked and furious as they read the new contract in the cafeteria. They now had to pay a substantial price for health care, which had previously been free after 18 months on the job. Their wages would be frozen with no increases for three years. And they got no relief from mandatory overtime that in the hot summer had them working 13-hour shifts day after day. The workers decided to go on strike. It was a wildcat strike—a throwback to a more radical past, when workers would often strike without authorization from the union leadership. It was early January, bitter cold, but they formed a picket line outside the plant. Police showed up and so did union officials, who encouraged workers to cross the picket line and go into the factory. A union official even told Robles that the police were there to protect the workers' right to cross the picket line and do their jobs. On the second day of the strike, the union chief steward crossed the line. Robles was disgusted. For more than two weeks they kept the picket line up, but each day more workers crossed it. The cold was brutal and the company was offering piecemeal raises and otherwise cajoling people to return to work. On a particularly frigid morning, some workers were lured across the picket line by the quintessential Chicago bait of Krispy Kreme doughnuts and coffee. A phalanx of Latino elected officials came to offer support to the strikers, including U.S. Congressman Luis Gutierrez, who made a speech from the back of a pickup truck. Robles remembers the Congressman saying he could not force the company to increase their wages, but he could raise his voice and shout, "Si se puede" (the common Spanish chant meaning "Yes we can!") Robles was not impressed. "Well, that's great," he scoffed. He wanted action. But on January 17, 2002, Robles remembers, the strike was declared a failure. He went back to work, but he and other disgruntled employees felt that they were only biding their time. They were determined to get rid of the union.

Robles and a few others had contacts at immigrants-rights and labor-rights groups around the city, so they sought out someone they thought could help: Martin Unzueta, an immigrant from Mexico City who worked for the United Network for Immigrant and Refugee Rights (UNIRR).

About a decade before, Unzueta had been dissatisfied with conditions at the Chicago printing press where he worked. After hearing a workers' rights presentation by the group now called Interfaith Worker Justice, he started organizing. For his efforts to form a union, he was fired. This was shortly after the landmark U.S. Supreme Court "Hoffman Plastics vs. NLRB" decision, which essentially ruled that undocumented immigrants do not have legal recourse if they are fired for union organizing. The decision was a huge blow to the immigrants'-rights and labor movements, coming at a time when unions were increasingly realizing the power and importance of immigrant workers. Labor and immigration lawyers called the decision illegal and unconstitutional. It meant that Unzueta could not fight for back wages or his job, claiming retaliation for the organizing activity which normally would have been protected by the National Labor Relations Act.

Unzueta began working for UNIRR, doing "Know Your Rights" presentations of his own for workers, telling them about federal agencies like OSHA and the Department of Labor and urging them not to let employers take advantage of them. His fifth presentation, and his largest audience to date, was for Republic workers. After his talk, he and the workers began to strategize about how to oust the CSJB and bring in a new union.

Several years earlier, the UE had run a bitterly fought, ultimately unsuccessful campaign to unionize Latino workers at Edsal, a company that made lockers, in the Back of the Yards neighborhood, which was once home to the city's famous meatpacking houses. The lead organizers were fired, and a complaint filed with the National Labor Relations Board (NLRB) claiming retaliation failed. One of the fired workers became a labor activist, collaborating with both the UE and Unzueta, and soon Unzueta was introducing UE organizers to the Republic workers. The UE's direct, activist attitude was a breath of fresh air to Robles and other workers who were sick of the CSJB's inaction and hostility. The workers decided to kick out the CSJB and bring in the UE.

This was late 2003, about a year before the CSJB's union contract would expire. The UE launched its typical organizing drive, holding meetings to inform workers of their rights, providing stickers and flyers, and pointing out all the things the CSJB was not doing for them. Robles remembers that for the first time, CSJB union officials actually showed up and attempted to convince workers they were helping them. Most weren't buying it. Meanwhile, company officials launched an aggressive campaign against the UE. Advised by an anti-union law firm, they held public meetings decrying unions. Meinster said they displayed large photos of the workers leading the UE drive, and said, "If you join the union, this person will control your life for the next three years." He also felt company officials tried to pit Latino and African American workers against each other, a common tactic in anti-union campaigns.

Republic managers utilized a typical carrot-and-stick approach to try to thwart the UE's efforts: along with intimidating key organizers and disparaging the UE, the company suddenly stocked the lunch room with Xbox video games and ping pong tables, built a basketball court outside, and even hosted cookouts for the workers. Robles said company officials begged the workers to give them a year to prove that workers could be happy without a union. They referred to the workers' well-known disillusionment with the CSJB and insinuated all unions were the same. Robles was afraid that many workers were buying the company's spiel, so he went into overdrive, talking to co-workers about the merits of the UE. He held meetings for the second-shift workers, often at St. Pius Church and the Casa Aztlan community center in Pilsen, the heart of the city's Latino activist scene, where many workers lived. He cornered co-workers for one-on-one talks in the cafeteria. Every week he handed out flyers. Getting a crash course in workers rights, he was surprised and elated to learn they had the right to wear pro-union stickers and buttons and pass out literature on the job.

When the vote came around on November 10, 2004, the UE won by a landslide. The UE got 340 votes, the organizers remember; the CSJB got 8 or 9, and just over 100 workers voted for no union.

UE Local 1110 was born.

Negotiations for a new contract began immediately. The UE drove a hard bargain, and it paid off. They obtained a nearly un-heard-of average $3-an-hour raise over the course of three years, with $1.75 in the first year. They overhauled a subpar bonus system. And they won the right to have 19 union stewards on the shop floor, compared to five before.[29] This meant more power for the union and more ability to file and win grievances. In contrast to the CSJB, which was run by officials who most union members never saw, the UE Local 1110 leadership was elected from among the workers themselves, who continued to work on the shop floor. For the first time, workers began to feel like they were equals to their supervisors. Robles was thrilled. When co-workers would come to him asking if the union could help them, he would say, "You are the union, I am the union, we are the union."

Melvin Maclin, by contrast, was not initially glad to be part of the UE. He almost voted against a union because he was so disillusioned with the CSJB and would have preferred not to be paying dues. But then he saw UE representative Leah Fried at work. Fried, a 36-year-old with fiery brown eyes and Betty Page bangs, had grown up learning about labor history from her own family. She grew up in Rogers Park, an eclectic lakeside neighborhood on Chicago's far north side known as a haven for activists and rabble-rousers. The nation's oldest labor press, Charles H. Kerr & Co., founded in 1886, is run out of a cluttered, sagging Rogers Park three-flat. Fried's father was the editor of his local union newsletter (AFSCME Council 31, which represents government employees from teachers to prison guards), and her mother helped organize a union at a large non-profit organization that serves refugees and immigrants. Before joining the UE 11 years earlier, Fried had worked a smorgasbord of jobs including truck driver, farm laborer, temporary office worker, social-service agency case manager, and community organizer. She married into a family of Guatemalan labor and human-rights activists, and her husband is a prominent organizer of workers centers nationwide. They would spend long nights debating and arguing about labor history and strategy. So when the idea for the occupation was hatched, Fried was ready. "She was on fire. The company hated her, which made us love her more," Maclin said. "I've always been a fighter. So I listened to Leah."

There were several lunchrooms in the factory. The one for Maclin's glass-cutting division did not have a refrigerator at the time, and under the CSJB, workers had been too disempowered and intimidated by management to demand one. So one day when then-owner Ron Spielman was walking by, Maclin stopped him and demanded a fridge. The lunchroom got a new refrigerator, and Maclin got his co-workers' admiration. After they joined the UE, they asked him to run for union office. He declined at the time, but a seed was planted. Soon a steward was fired for cursing out an unpopular supervisor, and "as fate would have it," in Maclin's words, he ended up filling the vacancy.

The organizing drive did not end with the union election. The union became locked in an ongoing battle with the company, fighting daily just to force supervisors to honor the contract they had signed. They launched campaigns in defense of grievances— when a worker was unfairly fired or disciplined, and when agreements about schedules or working conditions weren't respected. The workers would wear stickers and armbands, hold meetings, pass out flyers, march up to Spielman's and later Gillman's office or even to their homes.

"It's grassroots, the workers run the union," says Robles proudly. "With the CSJB, the union was just two people doing whatever the company wanted. But with the UE, we started getting training, finding out how to defend ourselves, that we have the same rights as the supervisors. The UE creates leaders."

A TALE OF TWO UNIONS

The CSJB and the UE are both "independent" unions that are not members of either the AFL-CIO or the Change to Win Coalition, formed when the SEIU, UNITE-HERE, and several other major unions split off from the AFL-CIO in 2005. But the CSJB and UE could be seen as polar-opposite ends of the organized labor spectrum.

The Central States Joint Board operates pension funds and a number of unions in Chicago. One of its former top officials, John Serpico, was infamous for connections to organized crime. A 1999 *Chicago Sun-Times* story described him thus:

> Serpico is the chairman of the Illinois International Port Authority, a position he has maintained under four Illinois governors despite his connections to top Chicago mobsters. He also has doled out hundreds of thousands of dollars in union campaign contributions to former governors James R. Thompson [...] Jim Edgar [...] Gov. Ryan, Mayor Daley and other politicians.[30]

In 2001, former CSJB president Serpico and then-president Maria Busillo were found guilty of charges including racketeering, conspiracy, bank fraud, wire fraud, and mail fraud. They had used the union's money to illegally influence banks to give them $5 million worth of loans that they wouldn't have gotten under normal circumstances, and otherwise used the financial clout of the union for their own gain.

In 1996, a northwest-side Chicago bank, Capitol Bank and Trust, was also found guilty of bribing the CSJB union officials with favorable loans in order to get millions in union deposits. The bank was fined $800,000 and placed on probation by federal authorities.[31]

In addition, Serpico and Busillo allegedly got multi-million-dollar kickbacks from a hotel construction scheme and payments for consulting and construction work that was never done. The government alleged that the two laundered the money, and that the illegal loans were used for purposes including launching a film studio with an alleged mobster and buying a condo in Florida.[32]

At the time of the indictment the CSJB represented about 20,000 workers affiliated mostly with the International Union of Allied Novelty and Production Workers (IUANPW), including manufacturing, chemical, metal, and plastics workers.

The CSJB is often described as a "company union" and accused of giving workers little or no say in the decisions made about their contract negotiations and campaigns. A 1999 U.S. Attorney's Office press release says: "CSJB entities did not regularly hold contested elections and Serpico and Busillo selected or controlled the selection of candidates who ran unopposed."

The UE, on the other hand, is famous for being run primarily by workers, like Robles and Maclin, who also serve as the local union officials.

The UE was formed in 1936 at a conference in Buffalo, New York, attended by independent local unions and non-unionized workers in radio and electrical manufacturing who had come together seeking to form a larger, progressive organization. They asked the American Federation of Labor (AFL) to recognize them, but the AFL turned them down. So the UE became the first union chartered by the newly-formed CIO (originally called the Committee of Industrial Organizations, later changed to Congress of Industrial Organizations).[33]

The AFL was a skilled craftsman's union, organized by trade rather than by workplace. The CIO, by contrast, was based on workplaces and embraced large groups of unskilled workers. The CIO was started by legendary United Mine Workers of America president John Lewis. It was interested in power in numbers, unlike the AFL unions' tendency toward exclusion in order to keep a monopoly on available jobs in the skilled trades. The two organizations were also split along racial lines. After World War II, Philadelphia, Detroit, and other industrial cities were torn by racial tension in the labor market. Black workers had filled previously white jobs during the war, but now returning white war vets wanted these jobs back. Meanwhile, black veterans also returning from the battlefield were furious at the prospect of being denied jobs after having fought for their country. The CIO often reached out to black workers, seeing this partly as a way to increase their ranks, while the AFL generally backed white (including ethnic Irish and Italian) workers who were terrified and irate at the prospect of competing with blacks for jobs. In Philadelphia, during a bitter strike of white transit workers resisting the federal government's mandate to integrate the workforce, the AFL lobbed slogans like "A vote for CIO is a vote for niggers on the job."[34]

Even though the CIO was more radical and militant than the AFL, in the 1940s it fell prey to the anti-Communist hysteria sweeping the nation. In 1947, Congress passed the viciously anti-union Taft-Hartley Act, which among many other things forced union officers to swear they were not Communists. At the end of World War II, the UE was the third-largest union in the CIO with half a million members, its largest locals at General Electric factories in Pennsylvania. Its bottom-up structure, progressive ideology, and various other political factors, however, caused CIO leaders and outside forces to label the UE a Communist union. In 1949, the UE withdrew from the CIO shortly before an anti-Communist purge wherein the CIO expelled 10 unions representing about a million members.[35]

During the anti-Communist witch hunts of the 1950s, politicians, CIO leaders, and business owners continued to attack and smear the UE in various ways, even trying to deport leader James Matles. Shop stewards were blacklisted and jailed, and the union ultimately lost about half its members. It slowly began to rebuild in the 1960s and '70s, but then the 1980s hit like a tsunami of outsourcing, off-shoring, deindustrialization, and general gutting of the American workforce—particularly the Midwestern workforce, which had previously seen it as their birthright to make the steel, autos, tractors, washing machines and other heavy objects that kept the country humming.

Chicago Tribune labor reporter Steve Franklin called the deindustrialization of the 1980s "America's secret earthquake, unparalleled devastation that went largely unnoticed as the rest of the country daydreamed and looked the other way."[36]

Automation meant plants needed fewer workers to profitably produce their goods. Cheaper labor in the largely non-union southern United States and even cheaper labor in Latin America and Asia meant plants were moving their factories elsewhere. And many large unions that had grown complacent or corrupt since their heyday of the 1930s apparently weren't putting up much of a fight as workers were forced to labor faster, longer, and harder for less pay.

One of the first and most famous labor travesties of that era was the 1977 layoffs of 4,100 workers at a steel mill in Youngstown, Ohio, known as "Black Monday." In the ensuing years, factories making everything from tires and textiles to washing machines and widgets were closing their doors or gutting their workforces at a rapid pace. Detroit, Milwaukee, Youngstown, and Akron, Ohio, were particularly hard hit, "hollowed out" in Franklin's words, as were smaller cities like Gary, Indiana, that went from thriving middle class enclaves to impoverished ghettoes almost overnight.

In 1982, 2,700 large-scale layoffs and plant closings wiped out more than 1.25 million blue-collar jobs across the United States. And for those who kept their jobs, things got markedly worse; a labor surplus gave employers new power in dictating terms and wages. In 1975, U.S. factory workers were the third-highest-paid in the developed world, but by 1991 they were only thirteenth, with average earnings of those who had not gone to college actually falling in real dollars over the 16-year span.[37]

By the 1990s, the Midwestern landscape was overtaken by deindustrialization, dotted by decrepit and mostly dismantled steel mills and factories. Warehouses and loading docks stood empty or sometimes were transformed into trendy condos and lofts.

Meanwhile, inner cities disintegrated into blocks upon blocks of vacant homes and weedy lots. The luckier or more enterprising municipalities (including Chicago) adapted, turning to tourism, information technology, science, or other sectors to survive. Given the breadth of the deindustrialization, some Chicagoans are now surprised to see factories like Republic remain, inconspicuously, in their midst.

And it is these small prizes that the UE has focused on, allowing the union to grow modestly during the 1990s, adding relatively small groups of workers here and there for a slow but steady gain in overall membership.

At this writing, the UE represents about 35,000 workers nationwide in private- and public-sector jobs, including a continued high concentration in manufacturing and specifically electrical manufacturing, metalworking, and plastics. Hence their base is still the type of manual labor that built strong unions of the past, and it continues to be an important though shrinking sector of the American workforce. The union's website says, "UE members work as plastic injection molders, tool and die makers, sheet metal workers, truck drivers, warehouse workers and custodians. We build locomotives, repair aircraft engines, assemble circuit boards, manufacture metal cabinets, produce industrial scales and make machine tools."

Like most unions, the UE has also branched out to workplaces beyond their traditional jurisdictions, and represents teachers, speech pathologists, nurses, clerical workers, graduate instructors, librarians, day-care workers, and even scientists.

In many cases these members chose to organize with the UE because of its progressive and independent nature, which makes it a good fit for workers who feel they don't fit into the traditional unions or who want their union to be part of a larger social movement.

In most large mainstream unions, top officials are likely to earn hundreds of thousands of dollars. But the UE's constitution caps top executives' pay to match the earnings of workers at the flagship GE plants in Pennsylvania. And staff organizers in any given industry—like Leah Fried and Mark Meinster—make no more than the top wage in that industry.

"It's hard to think (or act) like a big shot on a worker's wage," says the UE website. "We believe it's too easy for workers to develop boss-like points of view if they've become comfortable with boss-size salaries."

The decision-making structure of the UE is also quite different than other unions. As Andrew Dinkelaker, president of the UE eastern region, which covers the GE factories, notes:

> Most unions are top down—you have union bosses who can nix it if workers want to do a strike. The UE is set up democratically, so if its membership is interested and willing to take on a fight, the whole organization backs them and consults about the best way to achieve victory. It's not seen as the workers needing approval from the national organization. You hear these reports at other workplaces of members wanting to do something revolutionary but leadership stopping them. That's not the case within our

organizational structure. We don't have union bosses who
have the power to stop the workers. We try to figure out, if
there's motivation to fight, how do we become successful
rather than telling them no.

The UE was among the first unions to place its member organizing in a larger political context, opposing the Vietnam War and
fighting for women's rights and an end to racial discrimination.
It was also one of the first unions to embrace undocumented immigrant workers, who in decades past faced (and still face to some
extent) outright hostility from organized labor who saw them as
"stealing jobs" and as potential scabs. Furthering the relationship with Latino workers, the UE has a strategic partnership with
Mexico's independent FAT (*Frente Autentico del Trabajo*), or Authentic
Labor Front. This alliance grew out of both unions' opposition to
the North American Free Trade Agreement (NAFTA), which took
effect in 1994 and, as the unions predicted, has decimated jobs in
the United States and wreaked havoc on the Mexican economy.
The UE has also been involved in other international union solidarity efforts, including opposing the rampant murder of unionists
in Colombia. The south side of the UE building, a stocky brick
structure on Ashland Avenue's "Union Row," is emblazoned with
a mural celebrating the partnership with the FAT: an avant-garde
collage of clasped hands, cubist workers, and lightning bolts. Inside the musty 1960s-era building, social-realist murals painted in
the 1970s and evocative of Diego Rivera celebrate hard-toiling
workers locked in battle with corporate bosses. On one wall work-

ers labor in a blazing foundry, an image based on a real scene from Chicago's far south side. Above the stairwell leading into the UE's third floor offices, angry townspeople shake their fists at a gaggle of Klansmen and greedy businessmen who are literally sitting atop oppressed workers, pushing them down. In the corner is an image of a man shoving a gun into another's back, a depiction of the 1973 CIA-backed overthrow of Chilean president and socialist Salvador Allende. The words of the UE constitution crawl across the walls just below the ceiling.

An international perspective and independence from bureaucracy have helped the UE, relatively small as it is now, become a favorite union of Latino immigrants and an integral part of a burgeoning national immigrants'-rights movement.

On May 1, 2008, Republic workers were among thousands who marched through the city demanding meaningful immigration reform, part of a series of massive immigrants'-rights marches that swept through major cities and small towns nationwide. The first of these marches was in Chicago on March 10, 2006, launching a coalition called the March 10 Movement, which continues to be a major force for immigrants'-rights and other struggles. Republic workers including Robles are core members of this coalition.

Immigrants'-rights and labor struggles have dovetailed over the past few years, both as unions have embraced immigrant workforces, and as part of the rapid rise of the "workers center" movement, which brings together day laborers, temp workers, and workers at non-union sites.

In tough economic times, xenophobia historically rears its head and right-wing groups play on public fear and insecurity to stoke hatred of immigrants, who some see as taking jobs. But the truth is that immigrants are a huge and inextricable part of the U.S. labor force, so unions have stepped up organizing efforts of immigrant worksites, and also have realized it is in their interest to support struggles of workers' centers and other non-union groups of immigrant workers.

Large, powerful unions like the Service Employees International Union (SEIU) and the United Food and Commercial Workers (UFCW) have recognized the importance of Latino immigrants in keeping organized labor alive, and they have made a point of reaching out to these workers and largely immigrant workplaces. Latinos were a backbone of the SEIU's successful nationwide Justice for Janitors campaign, and the UFCW organizes workers at slaughterhouses and poultry plants, the vast majority of whom are Latino immigrants. But the UE has found a particular niche with smaller immigrant workplaces, especially light manufacturing like Republic, largely because of their close ties with immigrants'-rights activism. Another of UE's major campaigns in Chicago was winning the right to represent workers at the Azteca tortilla factory in Pilsen, the heart of the city's Mexican community.

The Azteca workers were originally represented by a "company union" run by a politically connected family, the Duffs, who were implicated in a major federal corruption investigation.[38] When their contract expired in 2002, the Azteca workers voted to decertify that union and join the UE. The union and company entered into highly contentious contract negotiations, in which the owner proposed to increase health insurance costs, eliminate seniority, end maternity leave, eliminate pay for clean-up time, alter the union's power to file grievances, and otherwise make things worse for the workers. The negotiations stalled, and the following months saw a campaign inside and outside the workplace. The UE lodged Unfair Labor Practice charges regarding Azteca's intimidation and harassment of pro-union workers, and supporters in Chicago and beyond raised awareness of the struggle. Workers and supporters handed out leaflets at supermarkets calling for a boycott of Azteca tortillas until the company met their demands for higher wages, better benefits, and improved conditions. On September 30, 2002, with the company still refusing to budge, most of the Azteca employees walked off the job. For the next seven months, more than 100 workers manned the picket lines, which Teamsters truck drivers refused to cross. The strike continued through the winter and the next spring. Eventually, the NLRB ruled on one Unfair Labor Practice charge in the workers' favor, and the union dropped other charges. With some concessions won from the company, on May 5, 2003 (Cinco de Mayo), the workers voted to end the strike but continue the boycott in an ongoing bid to pressure Azteca on their demands.[39]

© David Schalliol

CHAPTER THREE

SHUTTING THE DOOR ON REPUBLIC

In late November, there was some interesting news in the Midwestern window and door industry. Someone had purchased a window and door factory called TRACO (for Three Rivers Aluminum Company) in Red Oak, Iowa, a town of 6,200 in the southwest corner of the state, 50 miles from Omaha. The new owner was Echo Windows & Doors LLC, a company incorporated in Illinois on November 18 by Sharon Gillman, the wife of Republic owner Richard Gillman. The news was reported in a window and door industry trade journal and various Chicago and Iowa media, and the workers, soon found out.

Now it seemed clear where the machinery mysteriously leaving the Republic factory was headed. This development added insult to injury for the UE workers. Not only was the company apparently shutting down without giving them the benefit of an explanation; it appeared that the assets were being spirited away to continue business as usual somewhere else, and somewhere without a union.

On Tuesday, December 2, plant operations manager Tim Widner called Republic workers to a meeting in the cafeteria. He gave them the news that most had been expecting to hear for some weeks now: the plant was closing, and in just three days. They would not get severance pay, nor pay for their accrued vacation time. Many workers had deferred vacations specifically at managers' request, since fall is a busy season in the window industry. In all, the company owed almost $150,000 in vacation pay, with as much as $6,000 due some individual workers.[40] Widner blamed the closure on Bank of America "cutting off credit" to the company, and then made a quick getaway, telling workers they'd get their final paychecks on Friday, December 5, and would have health insurance through December 15.

Many of the workers headed directly over to the UE hall about two miles away to decide how to proceed. Their anger and anxiety over the prospect of losing their jobs—in such a harsh economy and so close to Christmas—was tempered by a rising sense of determination and excitement about what they were about to do. Workers were angry that owner Richard Gillman had not even ventured down from his office to break the news himself.

Around that time, Melvin Maclin remembers UE organizer Leah Fried saying, "If you guys let them close the doors Friday, that's it. Can you live with that?" "No," Maclin said to himself. The workers had been planning for a month to occupy the factory; now was the time to act on that plan. Maclin decided he would be part of it. It wasn't a decision he made lightly. As a young man he had made some bad choices and ended up in jail, an experience he never wanted to repeat. Now he was consciously making a move that could put him back behind bars. It wasn't easy convincing himself, and convincing his wife was even harder. "She thought I had lost my mind!" he said later. With six adult children and 16 young grandchildren looking forward to the holidays, Maclin felt like his family was on the line. "If we fight and lose, at least we'll know we fought," he told his wife. "It's about our dignity." By the end of the meeting, at least 30 other workers agreed with Maclin and promised to physically occupy the factory. Almost everyone else was ready to picket outside.

As soon as the meeting finished, union organizers began to strategically get word out to their allies and trusted advisers. C.J. Hawking, a minister connected to Interfaith Worker Justice, was one of the first to hear. Interfaith Worker Justice has a long history of tapping ministers, rabbis, imams and other spiritual leaders to persuade or shame the powers-that-be into doing the right thing. Hawking and solidarity organizers got on the phones and pulled together a rally and prayer vigil outside Bank of America's headquarters for the very next day. This would be the public launch of the strategy that had been germinating behind closed doors: they had been told Bank of America was to blame for the factory closing, so they would take their demands not to Gillman, but to the bank.

Meanwhile, UE western region president Carl Rosen was also busy spreading the news. He and U.S. Congressman Luis Gutierrez had been friends and fellow activists since the days of Harold Washington, Chicago's first African American mayor, whose 1983 election not only broke racial barriers but also was a historical upset of Chicago's Democratic machine. Since then Gutierrez's and Rosen's paths had crossed often in various movements and struggles. Since 1992, Gutierrez has represented the horseshoe-shaped congressional district that encompasses both Pilsen, the city's most prominent Mexican neighborhood, and Humboldt Park, the heart of the Puerto Rican community. Gutierrez, who is Puerto Rican, is well known for his advocacy for immigrants'-rights and not afraid to take a stand. He was vocal in the campaign to free Puerto Rican nationalists charged in the early 1980s with planning terrorist activities. He was arrested twice for protesting on the U.S. Navy's bombing practice range on the Puerto Rican island of Vieques, as part of a long-standing campaign to stop the military exercises. (Sixteen of the Puerto Rican prisoners' sentences were commuted by President Bill Clinton, and in 2003 the Navy did cease bombing on Vieques.) More recently, Gutierrez has hosted massive town-hall meetings where people give testimony about how immigration raids and deportations have torn their families apart.

So as soon as the factory occupation plans were underway, Rosen called Gutierrez and told him what was up. Many of the Republic workers live in Gutierrez' congressional district, and he remembered the factory from his visit during the wildcat strike.

Rosen also called another longtime ally and fellow activist, Chicago city councilman Ric Muñoz, who represents the Little

Village neighborhood, a vibrant southwest-side barrio of recent immigrants. Little Village's main drag, 26th Street, could easily be mistaken for a street in Mexico. Mariachis stroll from restaurant to restaurant, *norteño* music blares out of small record stores, vendors sell corn on the cob and pork skins from pushcarts, and at night men dressed to the nines cruise the streets in big cars as gang members throw menacing gestures at each other from the corners. Muñoz grew up in this neighborhood and knows well the struggles and spirit of hardworking Mexican immigrants. He and Rosen and other UE leaders worked closely together during a seminal grassroots struggle in 2001 to force the city to build a badly needed new high school in Little Village. Starting on Mother's Day of that year, about 40 mothers and grandmothers went on a hunger strike and camped out at the proposed site for the school, then just a rubble-strewn lot. Union members, activists and community groups adopted the struggle and became a constant presence. They gained national attention, and soon the school was built—a beautiful ecologically friendly building housing an innovative institution with a social-justice curriculum. As soon as Muñoz heard about the factory closing and the potential for direct action, the hunger strike came to mind. He is a firm believer that political victories come from a perfect storm of timing, moral authority, and community support, and Republic had the potential for all three.

On Wednesday, December 3, after the first shift, the union bused Republic workers downtown to the rally outside Bank of America's headquarters. It is an imposing and handsome building covering an entire block, built of smooth blonde stone decorated in the lacy curlicues and flourishes so common in the architecture of

Chicago's industrial glory days. Black-and-gold placards reading "Bank of America Building" top revolving doors trimmed in gold. Two large flags, one American and one white and emblazoned with Bank of America's logo, fly outside the building and also outside additional Bank of America offices one block north.

With her clerical collar on, Hawking led a prayer for justice against this backdrop as cab horns blared and pedestrians hurried by. After her prayer, Meinster approached Hawking and told her that civil disobedience might be in the works on Friday, the last day of work. Hawking immediately snapped into planning mode and started thinking about providing food and contacting reporters. But Friday is such a bad day for media attention, she lamented. Couldn't they reschedule? No, Meinster said, they'd have to make the best of it.

Rosen, Gutierrez, Muñoz, and a few other allies spent Wednesday strategizing and researching. As the workers were planning their occupation, they were trying to determine what laws might have been broken by closing the factory and what political pressure points might be probed. They gave themselves a crash course in the Worker Adjustment and Retraining Notification (WARN) Act.

During the waves of plant closings in the 1980s, unions, even in their weakened state, demanded laws preventing or regulating plant closings. The WARN Act was passed in this period as something of a compromise, backed by Republicans and Southern Democrats, who wanted Northern and Midwestern plants to be able to close and send the jobs south.[41] The law basically says when an employer with more than 100 employees is going to close or make significant layoffs, the employer must give the workers 60 days' notice.[42] Theoretically, government agencies or other parties would also step in to offer retraining—the R part of WARN—for the employees, though labor experts say this rarely happens. If the employees are not given 60 days' notice, they are owed up to 60 days' severance pay. But there are exceptions to the law, including for unforeseeable business occurrences, natural disasters, or a "faltering company." This could be cut and dried in the case of something like a tornado or fire that destroys a business. But there is usually much more of a gray area: trying to define if the effects of an economic crisis or failing industry are "foreseeable" occurrences. Another exception to the law allows the employer to avoid giving notice if an announcement would hurt the business, with lenders or customers fleeing a sinking ship. (This would apply mainly in the case of mass layoffs, when the business doesn't actually plan to close). If an employer claims this exception, workers must prove that the business was already doomed or that customers would have been lost regardless of the WARN Act notice. The Act also offers employers a "Get out of jail free" card, as one attorney described it, if they claim they tried in good faith to comply with the act and somehow were prevented from doing so. The law is often described by labor lawyers as toothless, since employers who break it face only minimal punitive damages of up to $500 a day until workers are paid.[43] The law is routinely broken, and employers often get away with violations without facing legal action. Any litigation is likely to be lengthy and financially draining for the workers, ending with at most a slap on the wrist for employers. Critics charged Bank of America with trying to subvert the WARN Act as it laid off its own employees during the first few months of 2009, part of the three-year, 30,000-plus job cuts it had announced in late 2008. By laying people off in small groups, the bank avoided triggering the "mass lay-off" component of the WARN Act in most cases.[44]

Problematic as the WARN Act might be, Gutierrez, Rosen, and the local union leaders seized on the law as an important part of their strategy. They said that Republic had clearly violated the WARN Act, though in court Republic could easily have claimed it was a "faltering company" and probably would have invoked "unforeseeable business circumstances." In keeping with their larger strategy, Gutierrez and Rosen would connect Bank of America with the WARN Act violation. Gillman himself was doing as much. He had already told union leaders that he asked Bank of America to authorize him to give the employees WARN Act notice, and, he said, bank officials said no.[45] In a statement to the media, he said he asked Bank of America in October for permission to begin WARN Act compliance, and was denied.[46] Bank of America's Pat Holden later said no such conversation ever took place, and she stressed that the bank had neither authority nor obligation to "authorize" any of the company's actions or in any way tell the company what to do.[47]

Aside from studying possible violations of the WARN Act, the union strategists and their allies also discussed how the timing was right for a bold and historical workplace action. With many thousands of people nationwide out of work or fearing for their jobs—including middle-class and skilled workers who had never expected to find themselves among the unemployed—public sentiment was likely to be on the side of workers more than at any time in the recent past. While two years ago citizens might have scorned an action that seemed to violate a company's rights or the sanctity of private property, now many were disgusted with corporations and banks and longing for an underdog willing to stand up to them. A factory takeover would be just the thing.

The UE members frequently invoked the UAW sit-down strikes in relation to their occupation. But in reality the parallel was a stretch, and the UE workers actually had a much bigger challenge ahead of them. The UAW strikes were not related to plant closings, but rather were militant strikes demanding better wages, security, benefits, and the right to unionize.[48] Ford, General Motors, Chrysler, Bendix, and the other auto plants needed to keep their production lines running in the 1930s; feeding the market and reeling in their profits depended upon it. The same was true for the 1989 Pittston mine strike in Virginia, where union miners and supporters essentially took over and prevented scabs from working by blocking company coal trucks and mine entrances.[49]

The miners and auto workers exerted great leverage by taking over the mines or plants and withholding their labor. But at Republic, the owner and creditors did not want the workers to work, and they had no immediate use for the factory or machinery (except in the Iowa facility). The Republic situation actually had more in common with the famous factory takeovers in Argentina following the country's 2001 economic collapse. Tens of thousands of workers took over idle factories that had made everything from auto parts to leather to chocolate and ran the companies themselves, raising money to fix broken equipment and finding eager customers in a country enamored of populist struggle.[50] But Chicago is not Buenos Aires. Argentina's economy had been thrown into chaos that makes the United States' current situation pale by comparison, and in Argentina, militant action and protest are woven into the social and political fabric.

So the Republic workers' factory occupation would only really have leverage in relation to their taking temporary possession of the assets in the building—the finished windows and doors and raw materials stacked there, and the machinery that had not yet been removed. More importantly than this leverage, though, they would have the power of spectacle and opinion.

In a sense, they would be running what is known as a "corporate campaign," a specific strategy that became popular in the 1980s as unions got increasingly desperate and when the traditional methods like strikes and work slowdowns either weren't working or top union bureaucrats were unwilling to deploy them. During a corporate campaign, an employer is targeted on multiple fronts through its board of directors, shareholders, customers, and contractors. The corporate campaign brings the labor struggle into the community, with the union courting public support and pressuring the employer through its public image and consumer base. Perhaps the most famous architect of these campaigns was a scrappy, stocky, ruggedly handsome New Yorker named Roy Rogers, whose high-profile entry into local struggles was often highly divisive.[51] In the past decade, corporate campaigns have also become popular and successful in situations and sectors not conducive to traditional union organizing, including by non-unionized migrant farm workers and temporary laborers who don't have one steady employer. The Coalition of Immokalee Workers in southern Florida has used such tactics to gain important improvements for the immigrant workers who toil picking tomatoes in the steamy south. They have forced agricultural growers to make concessions by publicly targeting their buyers: Taco Bell, Burger King, and McDonald's, among others.

Immigrant farmworkers in the south often labor in horrendous conditions, are paid little, are exposed to toxic chemicals, and in some cases are even held in de facto slavery. The Immokalee Workers knew it would be hard to target the various small and sometimes fly-by-night vegetable-growing companies who employed the workers. But the corporations who buy tomatoes and other produce from these growers are international brand names. Even though—as with Bank of America—Taco Bell and other restaurants have no legal obligation to the tomato pickers, a series of store boycotts, rallies, and tours targeting Taco Bell nationwide forced the company, and later other fast-food chains, to demand better pay and working conditions in the fields.[52] As with the Immokalee Workers, the Republic workers chose to focus not so much on their direct nemesis (the company itself) but rather on an indirect player (Bank of America) that had much more at stake.

On Wednesday and Thursday, December 3 and 4, the workers discussed the details of their campaign. The conversations involved close allies and union leaders, who made cryptic calls to loyal supporters hinting that they should be ready for a big action on Friday: something historic, something that hadn't happened since the 1930s.

Representative Luis Gutierrez, D-Ill. speaks during a rally at
the Republic Windows factory on Saturday, Dec. 6, 2008.
(AP Photo/Brian Kersey)

CHAPTER FOUR

THE REVOLT

FRENETIC FRIDAY

Company officials had told the workers to report at 9 a.m. on Friday, December 2, three hours after their normal start time. Gillman and other executives met with union leaders at 8 a.m. The union had urged workers not to have any contact with management until after they had a chance to huddle with the union. The company had the workers' paychecks ready, but they also had more bad news: health benefits, which they had said would last until December 15, had actually already been cut off, not even giving workers a chance to squeeze in a last doctor's visit.

When Robles, Meinster, Fried, and the other union leaders met with the full workforce, they quickly called for a vote on whether to enact their plan: the factory occupation. Hands shot up enthusiastically and people cheered and shouted "Si se puede." It was unanimous. Young Republic COO Barry Dubin was given the task of handing out personalized folders to workers: each folder contained a letter of recommendation, information on unemployment benefits, and a few inconsequential pieces of paper; a painful parting gift after years of service. He met the workers in the same cafeteria where on Tuesday operations manager, Tim Widner, had given them official word of the plant closing. The setting was oddly appropriate—mustard-yellow Formica tables harkening back to the factory's heyday decades before; unused commercial kitchen appliances left over from when the cafeteria used to actually dish up hot lunches. Now, dusty vending machines offered the only sustenance. The workers were so angry that Meinster said union leaders firmly pleaded with them to make sure Dubin "got out in one piece." He did, and the workers began their occupation.

They saw Dubin leave the plant around 1:30 p.m. Republic officials were supposed to show up at a 4 p.m. meeting at Bank of America organized by Congressman Gutierrez, but none appeared. Union leaders think bank officials and the Republic executives had agreed that Republic should be a no-show to stretch the negotiations into the next week. Meanwhile union members and their supporters had been calling local and national reporters. The press, many already familiar with the issue from Wednesday's vigil and rally outside Bank of America, embraced the story as a perfect example of the latest grim unemployment numbers released by the government. "They were seeing it as a plant-closing story, they couldn't grasp that it was a factory occupation, because that's not something we ever have here," said Leah Fried. By late afternoon, Congressman Gutierrez and the union members had returned from the meeting at the bank, made fruitless by the company's absence. Now came the moment of truth. The handful of Republic supervisors who were in the office Friday had told the workers they had to be out by 5 p.m. Would they disobey these orders and push on to a full-blown factory occupation? They took the final vote. Again, it was unanimous, and the cheers and chants were even louder than before. While previously about 30 people had vowed to occupy the plant, suddenly everyone wanted to do it, arrest risk be damned.

Journalists swarmed around Congressman Gutierrez as he exited the factory that Friday evening. One called out to ask whether the occupation was illegal. After all, the workers were camped out on private property without the permission of the owner. Gutierrez didn't miss a beat. He shot back that the workers had ownership of the assets as the fruits of their labor. "It takes two things to make that window—parts and labor," he explained later. "To the extent the labor hasn't been paid for, those windows belong to the workers. If a plumber fixes my toilet and I don't pay him, he can take out a lien. The workers don't trust the courts, so their lien is their bodies."

The workers swung into action, forming committees and making plans. Their occupation would be a strictly nonviolent and orderly one, aimed at protecting the assets that they viewed as their own, as Gutierrez had explained. They decided that only 30 to 40 workers would actually be inside the factory at any given time, and they would rotate in and out in shifts. Only workers and union staff and some family members would be allowed on the shop floor. Keeping the place safe and tidy was important to both their public image and their hopes of reopening the plant. Several workers posted themselves as guards at the doors between the shop floor and the lobby, holding back eager reporters and activists trying to finagle a peek inside. One reporter convinced Robles' young son Oscar to take her camera inside and snap photos. "She brainwashed my son!" joked Robles' wife, Patricia. The workers organized teams to do everything from cleaning the bathrooms to providing security to shoveling snow.[53]

"People were just excited to be doing what it took," remembers Meinster. "They had been working there for decades, and to be thrown out in the cold without a job right before Christmas, it was a slap in the face. We couldn't have gotten people out of there if we'd wanted to."

That evening, factory managers did call the police demanding that the workers be forcibly removed. But the union was one step ahead. City Councilman Muñoz had called his friend Scott Waguespack, the city councilman representing Goose Island and the surrounding area. Waguespack, formerly a Peace Corps volunteer in Kenya, had been recently elected with a platform of revitalizing local industry. At Muñoz' urging he had called the local police commander that morning to give him a heads-up, and to explain that this was a labor-management dispute in which the police should not intervene. Waguespack said the local beat cops, union members themselves, were happy to comply.

MARSHALLING THE TROOPS

Jerry Mead-Lucero could be considered a labor geek.

He hosts a labor radio show for an organization housed in the same building as the UE headquarters. He writes long articles about local contract battles and he leads labor history tours in the Pilsen neighborhood, where many a struggle has begun. During the week, UE organizer Mark Meinster had called him with the tip that something would be happening on Friday. Mead-Lucero left work early that afternoon and headed over to the factory. The rumors he had heard were true; the workers were indeed occupying the plant. He joined the gaggle of journalists—including correspondents for *Le Monde*, Al-Jazeera, and other national and foreign media—and began interviewing supporters and members of other unions.

An hour or two after Mead-Lucero arrived, the workers emerged from the back of the factory to announce their decision to occupy the plant indefinitely until their demands were met. "It was just electrifying!" remembers Mead-Lucero. He immediately switched hats, putting away his voice recorder and taking out his cell phone to start organizing. Within minutes he was making calls to other union and labor activists, telling them to get down to the plant. "Some of the real journalists around me kind of flipped out, they thought I was one of them and now I had switched to activism," he remembers. "I realized this was something big and we had to mobilize community support."

One of Mead-Lucero's first calls was to minister C.J. Hawking. She was at a gala for the Illinois Labor History Society, titled appropriately "A New Deal for Workers: Past, Present, Future." She jumped up to the microphone; she couldn't have asked for a more enthusiastic audience. "You have a room full of labor historians, and labor history is being made," she remembers. "There was a collective gasp of excitement."

Mead-Lucero also called his wife, Claudia, an organizer in the immigrants'-rights movement, to get the word out to the Mexican hometown federations, the social and political clubs in Chicago and other U.S. cities that represent people from certain towns or states in Mexico. Then he rushed over to meet Claudia at a benefit dinner for the Latino Union grassroots organization, which was taking place on the second-floor ballroom of a bedraggled but grand old building on the city's northwest side. As a Mexican band was setting up for a dance later that night, he and Claudia climbed onto the stage to break the news about the factory occupation. A ripple of bewilderment and excitement spread through the room.

Conveniently, Mead-Lucero had also just recently signed up for Facebook, and his post about the factory occupation including his cell phone number spread like crazy through social networking. That night, he got a call at 3 a.m. from someone asking how they could support the workers, and starting early in the morning and throughout the weekend the calls continued nearly nonstop, including one from Argentina and one from the office of the

Reverend Jesse Jackson, who would visit the factory on Sunday. Mead-Lucero recorded a voice-mail message directing people to his website for the latest on the occupation.

Meanwhile, Congressman Gutierrez had a far swankier destination after leaving the factory Friday evening. He headed to a fundraiser for then-governor Rod Blagojevich. It was a questionable decision, as just that morning *The Chicago Tribune* had published a damning story about the FBI searching pharmacies owned by key Blagojevich donors as part of an ongoing federal corruption investigation.[54] Gutierrez was among those hoping to be appointed by the governor to the U.S. Senate seat vacated by Barack Obama; the feds were investigating what various people might be willing to do to get that Senate seat. Helping to raise funds for Blagojevich at that moment was not exactly a politically smart thing to do. But Gutierrez says his sole motivation in going to the fundraiser was to corner Blagojevich about Republic.

Gutierrez was scheduled to leave that week for a family trip to Puerto Rico, but he knew he had to stay in icy Chicago until the struggle was over. When Rosen called him, he thought, "Why can't we ever have problems in the spring and summer!"

A LONG WEEKEND

On Saturday, December 6, a hastily organized support rally attracted several hundred people. Donations of food, blankets, pillows, sleeping bags, and other necessities poured into the factory. Over the weekend, Congressman Gutierrez returned to the factory several times, watching the occupation blossom into an international news story. He got a lot of media time, so people called him with updates and tips. He felt like a reporter breaking a big story. Though he declined to give names or details, he later said that various people approached him with documents that shed light on the Republic situation. One of these documents, he said, was a report from an independent financial consultant present at an October meeting at which Bank of America representatives and Gillman discussed options for liquidating the company. Several possible scenarios were proposed, Gutierrez said, and one of the items on the agenda was whether or how to comply with the WARN Act. This revelation irked the congressman. He recognized that Bank of America did not have a legal responsibility to make sure Gillman complied with the WARN Act, but he was angered by the fact that the bank was aware of the impending liquidation and the WARN Act and didn't somehow push Gillman to comply. At that point, Gutierrez noted, WARN Act compliance would have been as simple as notifying the workers that the factory was closing, so they would have 60 days to find another job. The Act doesn't explicitly mandate severance pay; only 60 days' notice—or severance pay if notice is not given. And of course Gutierrez was well aware that Bank of America had just received $25 billion in TARP bailout funds, the specifics of which were publicly hammered out in Congress. He explained:

> While not sanctioned in law, certainly from a public opinion standpoint and a corporate citizen point of view

Bank of America had not fulfilled its responsibility to the workers. And then with the bailout, those workers and all Americans became shareholders in Bank of America. While I understand they didn't have a legal responsibility, the issue of the WARN Act was raised and they didn't do anything about it. If you are taking the public's money, you should do a better job.

Gutierrez was a member of the House Financial Services Committee in Congress, and he had no qualms about throwing this weight around. He called committee chair Barney Frank (D-Mass.) asking for advice and staff resources, and, he says he threatened to subpoena various witnesses and documents regarding that October meeting and other financial dealings if bank officials did not cooperate. And Gutierrez was far from the only politician or public figure taking an interest in Republic. A labor expert from the Illinois Attorney General's office kept tabs on the situation over the weekend and reported back to his boss, Attorney General Lisa Madigan, who said she was eager to help the workers. On Sunday, she launched an investigation into whether Republic had broken state laws in regard to its workers or customers with unfilled orders. Her staff soon realized workers had not been paid for their last week of work, and it was unclear whether the company planned to pay them. "It looked like Gillman was going to worm out of it," said UE organizer Meinster. This could have been a serious and possibly criminal matter which the attorney general's office was investigating, though it became a moot point

Workers and supporters at the Republic factory.
(Photo © Anna Karewicz)

Illinois Governor Rod Blagojevich stands with workers on the fourth day of a sit-in at Republic. Blagojevich ordered all state agencies to stop doing business with Bank of America to try to pressure the bank into helping the laid-off workers. Blagojevich's appearance at Republic was his last before being indicted on massive corruption charges. (AP Photo/M. Spencer Green)

Workers inside the Republic factory.
(Photo © Anna Karewicz)

A UE union protest in front of the Bank of America
building on La Salle Street in Chicago. © Anna Karewicz

later when Gillman agreed to spend $117,000 of his own money to pay the workers.[55]

Also on Sunday, the Reverend Jesse Jackson visited the factory to hand out turkeys and offer encouragement. Patricia Robles and the kids snapped photos with him. U.S. Congresswoman Jan Schakowsky, a liberal who represents Chicago's north side lakefront, also made an appearance. Then they got an endorsement that made all the others pale.

A TV in the factory cafeteria where the workers were gathered was tuned to a press conference given Sunday afternoon by President-Elect Barack Obama. A reporter asked Obama what he thought of the factory occupation. "When it comes to the situation here in Chicago with the workers who are asking for the benefits and payments that they have earned, I think they're absolutely right," he said. "These workers, if they have earned these benefits and their pay, these companies need to follow through on their commitments."

A wild cheer went up. Robles thinks Obama's support was a turning point. During Friday's meeting, he had felt that Bank of America representatives and other powerful people "treated us like we were nobody, like we were stupid, like we stink." By Monday, it was a different story. The most respected man in the world had spoken up for them, and now Robles felt like the people in suits and high-rise office buildings saw them in a new light.

MANIC MONDAY

Monday morning, December 8, Governor Rod Blagojevich—not to be outdone by Obama—paid a visit to the factory. The governor had long fancied himself a hero of the working man. The son of Serbian immigrants, he often described growing up in blue-collar Chicago neighborhoods. He had gained deep support in working-class and immigrant communities for expanding healthcare to low-income families and helping people buy cheap prescription drugs from Canada, though his many critics attacked these programs as inefficient, unworkably expensive, and even illegal. Especially in a dire economy, championing the Republic workers was a public relations bonanza for Blagojevich. And he needed one. His political foes had long been calling for his impeachment; a number of his associates had been arrested in the past year as part of a sweeping federal corruption probe; and even among regular people his popularity had plummeted. After the damning *Chicago Tribune* story the previous Friday, the noose was tightening around the governor's neck. But at Republic, he appeared lively, cocky, and cheerful as ever. His famous mop of Elvis-inspired hair hung boyishly in his face, and his eyes sparkled as he declared his support for the workers.

Reporters seized the opportunity to question him about the corruption investigation. "I don't believe there's any cloud that hangs over me," Blagojevich declared. He couldn't stop himself:

I think there's nothing but sunshine hanging over me. I appreciate anybody who wants to tape me openly and notoriously and those who feel like they want to sneakily wear taping devices, I would remind them it kind of smells like Nixon and Watergate. Whatever I say is always lawful. The things I'm interested in doing are always lawful. If there are any things like that out there, the only things you'll hear are a governor who tirelessly and endlessly figures out ways to help average and ordinary working people.

Standing just behind his shoulder, city councilman Ric Muñoz chuckled. Armando Robles looked serious with his navy-blue union ball cap perched high on his head. Right next to Blagojevich stood another earnest union member with a picket sign held together with duct tape. Blagojevich teased Muñoz for losing $100 on an Oscar de la Hoya boxing match. Then he called boldly upon state agencies to stop any business with Bank of America until it "gave back" some of the bailout money to the Republic workers. The crowd cheered and erupted in chants of "Save more jobs" and "*Si se puede.*"

Watching over the scene was a giant inflatable rat with bloodshot eyes, a common presence at pickets nationwide. The rat was surrounded by burly Irish American and Italian American union members—truckers, pipefitters, and the like, proudly sporting their union caps and jackets. You could call them the old-school face of unionism. But here they were ecstatic to be declaring their support for black- and brown-skinned workers, mostly immigrants—the new face of unionism. Instead of seeing them as a threat, the old-schoolers saw them as an inspiration.

After Blagojevich left, more politicians took center stage, including U.S. Senator Dick Durbin. A few hours later downtown at City Hall, yet more elected officials weighed in. City councilman Joe Moore, a longtime progressive and antiwar activist from the north-side neighborhood of Rogers Park, matched Blagojevich and raised him one. He promised to introduce a city council ordinance not only ending city business with Bank of America, but also denying zoning changes requested for any Bank of America or subsidiary branch and preventing the bank from selling city bonds. Moore described the bailout funds as "money that was intended to jump-start the credit system and increase the number of loans to companies like Republic. But Bank of America, like other banks, is using that money not to increase loans but buy other assets.

"Bank of America is thumbing its nose at Congress and the public by taking federal loans while refusing to extend credit to a small manufacturing company with a long history of profitability," Moore continued. Republic's recent history was of course far from profitable, but the whole story was quickly gaining a nearly mythic momentum. "Rather than help workers, their families and the city's economy with the taxpayer money given to it, Bank of America is instead using the money to expand its financial empire," said Moore indignantly. Perhaps caught up in the moment and subconsciously harkening back 20 years, he later erroneously referred to Republic as "Republic Steel." Meanwhile that same day county commissioner Mike Quigley, who would later be elected to the U.S. Congress in a special election to fill the seat vacated by Obama's new chief of staff Rahm Emanuel, also promised to cut off county business with Bank of America until they did right by the Republic workers. In short, all the politicians were on board, and tripping over each other to see who could be most supportive of the workers and most indignant about the supposed evil of Bank of America.

Another meeting was called for Monday evening, December 8, at Bank of America's headquarters. In advance, Gutierrez huddled with two city councilman, Ric Muñoz and Billy Ocasio, who represents the largely Puerto Rican neighborhood of Humboldt Park. They met in Ocasio's office. It felt like the old days when independent politicians would band together to fight the Democratic machine, with which they had now mostly made peace. When the three got over to Bank of America, Gutierrez was annoyed to see more people than he'd expected: representatives from the city treasurer's office, the Chamber of Commerce, and other agencies and interest groups. He felt like Bank of America had invited these guests to "dilute the chances of success for the workers" and make bold action more difficult. Too many cooks, he called it. "It's human nature that you have a harder time reaching consensus the more people there are in the room," he said. "I said, 'Don't anybody leave, but your presence here is suspect until I see your actions.' The meeting didn't start out real well."

A Chamber of Commerce official asked the workers to tone down their statements to the media, to stop making the bank look bad. Maclin and Robles were furious that a businessman would try to silence them. Maclin slammed his fist down on the table and cursed loudly, vowing he would tell the media whatever he wanted. There was no resolution that night, though things seemed to be moving along despite the rocky start. Gutierrez stopped by the factory to promise the workers—and a crowd of TV cameras— that a proposal was in the works. Meanwhile, as the sun set Monday evening and a frigid slushy rain began to fall, a semi-truck pulled up outside the factory and disgorged bags of food, an effort Gutierrez had coordinated. He considered his donation more appropriate than the turkeys brought by Reverend Jackson. "You need something you can freeze, turkeys are too big," he noted. "And these are mostly Latinos, they don't eat a lot of turkeys. I got together chicken, rice, beans, tortillas, tomatoes, onions, the things in my refrigerator."

As fires blazed out of several trash drums, workers and supporters formed a line to throw the bags of food hand to hand from the truck up the sidewalk through the crowd into the factory, a lively exercise accompanied by much chanting and cheering. The workers' moods were balanced on a precipice between elated at the attention and grim, given the harsh reality they could be facing. Worker Apolinar Cabrera was surprisingly upbeat and hopeful, given his family's situation. His wife was pregnant, due sometime around Christmas day. Now they could be without health insurance, not to mention money for Christmas dinner and gifts for their children.

Friends William Lane and Donte Watson had thought they would spend their lives working at the company and retire from it. They had been reading and hearing about layoffs around the country but always felt that their jobs were safe. After all, people will always need replacement windows. Watson, wearing a brown White Sox ball cap and puffy coat with a furry collar, was not very involved in the union and rarely went to meetings; he said he'd been shocked when they got the news. He depended on his wages to support his six-year-old son. "My son knew there was a problem when I wasn't going to work in the morning," says Watson, 30. "It was hard to tell him, I had to break it down for him in a way he could understand."

Lane, 33, said his 11-year-old daughter didn't understand what was going on. "She's still asking for money and talking about Christmas," he said. "I had to say there will be no Christmas. We are truly shocked and scared. With this economic crisis there is nowhere to turn. I have extensive bills, a car note that I can't pay now, all the daily expenses. If they don't do the right thing I don't know what I'll do."

Watson felt betrayed by the company because he was proud of all the effort he had put into this job for eight years. He was angry that the company had closed with orders still to fill, because he didn't want customers to be let down. "People put their blood, sweat and tears into this company, it was our company too, not just the owners'," he said. "They knew this was coming and they didn't say a word to us. They owed us more respect than that. We don't want anything extra, we just want what we are owed."

Forty-one-year-old Dagoberto Cervantes ruefully noted that a solution must be reached soon, or never. He was encouraged and elated by all the public support and media attention, but he worried it would fade as the holidays approached. "It's now or never," he said in Spanish, grabbing the jacket hood of his five-year-old son, who was hopping precariously around on a small brick wall holding a picket sign. "*Es muy feo*"—"it's very ugly,"—said his son in a sweet little voice. Cervantes also has a 13-year-old daughter and was worried he wouldn't be able to get another job to support them if Republic remained closed. "We need money to pay the rent, to support our kids, all the things you need to survive," he said. "With this economic crisis and unemployment, there are no other jobs."

That's also how Jose Ornelas felt. An immigrant from Jalisco, Ornelas, 47, said his kids and wife were proud of him for taking part in the sit-in; though when his daughter first heard about the situation on the news, she thought her father had been kidnapped. "It's bad," he said. "A lot of companies are laying off—I don't know where we will get other work." He had only worked at one other factory in the United States in his three decades here, and that was only for two months.

"I hope we get some justice," said Ron Bender, a 55-year-old worker with 14 years at the plant and a laid-back, nonchalant attitude despite the drama around him. He hadn't seen anything like this since the protests of the 1960s and '70s that had defined his youth. "We have worldwide support, workers have been stepped on for so long...maybe this will set a precedent that corporate America can't just take advantage of regular people."

Elisa Romo, 46, was nervous about speaking to reporters but wanted to get the story out. Wearing fragrant perfume and a warm, shy smile, she described how her son in the Army was so proud of his mother taking part in this struggle. She is a single mother of four sons, though only one, age eight, still lives at home. "They all studied and went to college, so they'll have a better life than me," she said proudly of her older sons. Her eight-year-old spent two nights at the sit-in with her, telling press, "I'm here to help my mom." She felt like she was fighting for him. "They give all this money to banks, but they won't help the regular people," added Romo, her shyness giving way to anger. We don't want anything that isn't ours, we just want what's owed us."

As the crowd dispersed, the exhausted workers staying for the "night shift" retreated onto the shop floor, followed by a priest carrying purple vestments and a plastic container of communion wafers for an impromptu mass.

Officials at Bank of America still seemed blindsided by the whole situation. They avoided talking to media, just putting out a terse written statement saying that the bank had no role in telling the company how to run its business. "The bottom line is that TARP or no TARP, we have to remain firm in prudent stewardship of our resources," said Bank of America spokesperson Julie Westermann later. "Our shareholders, which now include taxpayers (thanks to the bailout), would not be served by throwing money at a company that can't repay the loan."

That night, the occupation was on TV screens across the country. On MSNBC's *Hardball*, Congressman Jan Schakowsky vowed to send a letter to the U.S. Treasury saying, "Look, if we can give that kind of money to Bank of America then we ought to be able to bail out these workers and this plant for exactly the kind of jobs we need."

She put the squeeze on both the government and the bank, telling *Hardball* host Chris Matthews, "Bank of America could come out smelling like a rose if for a fraction, a tiny tiny fraction of the money they've gotten, they extend this credit . . . This is 300 jobs and thousands of family members." MSNBC talk show host Rachel Maddow featured a long segment with former Merrill Lynch head John Thain's extravagance as a launching pad. "Perhaps Mr. Thain has not heard of the plight of Republic Windows & Doors in Chicago," she perkily opined. "Mr. Thain's $10 million bonus would be just what the doctor ordered to keep Republic's doors open; or it would make things about $33,000 easier for each of the 300 or so Republic workers who were laid off with almost no notice last week." Even on Fox TV, usually not considered a friend of labor, commentators lauded the workers. The media was eating out of the workers' hands.

TUMULTUOUS TUESDAY

Shortly after 6 a.m. on Tuesday, December 9, federal agents called Governor Rod Blagojevich to inform him that they were outside his home waiting to arrest him. The governor donned tight running pants, sneakers, and a Nike running jacket, and headed out to face the music: charges that he tried to sell Obama's Senate seat to the highest bidder, tried to force the firing of critical editors at *The Chicago Tribune*, and threatened to withhold funding from a children's hospital if an executive didn't cough up campaign donations, among other things. His lovingly crafted image of the selfless champion of the little guy was about to be swept away in a scandal that would see him impeached and likely facing prison time.

Meanwhile, over at Republic, the workers who had cheered Blagojevich less than 24 hours earlier heard news of his arrest but had more immediate things to worry about. The day started badly, as police had towed all the cars along Hickory Street in front of the factory. An officer told the union it was to make room for media vans, but the union suspected that wasn't the real story. There was hardly a reporter in sight anyway, since Blagojevich's arrest was making headlines worldwide. Workers noticed people they didn't recognize lurking around; they didn't like the looks of it. With people getting exhausted and increasingly nervous about the outcome of that day's negotiations and the actions of police, it was shaping up to be a rough day. The union sent out e-mails and text messages asking supporters to come out in force, and luckily many answered the call. That helped lift flagging spirits.

At 1 p.m., negotiators gathered again around a large table in a Bank of America conference room: politicians and government agency reps, Bank of America officials, the union leaders, Gillman, and a slew of lawyers. Robles remembers it as a big marble table, with at least 40 chairs. The talks were freewheeling and by turns conciliatory and contentious.

Maclin got the distinct impression that Bank of America officials were not so much concerned about the money being demanded of them as they were by the precedent-setting potential of the whole situation. "It's like they thought if we are fighting back and we win, then everyone will want to fight back," he said. "You could read that on their faces and hear it in their little comments. They were trying to make it sound like this was all *our* fault, complaining about how much money they had lost."

Gillman was already not the most popular person in the room, needless to say. But that afternoon he managed to turn the crowd even more steadfastly against him. According to various participants, he asked Bank of America that any new loan include severance pay for himself . . . and funds to pay the leases on two luxury cars.

"He said he'd received the same 'bonus' the previous year, which was interesting since that was the year they lost five million dollars," said the bank's Pat Holden. "He wasn't interested in paying the workers so much as in what he was getting out of this."

"We got a little hostile," remembered Gutierrez, grinning at his understatement. "When you have two hundred workers waiting to be paid . . . it takes a lot of gall to do something like that."

"We couldn't believe he asked for that," Maclin remembers. "Even his own attorney looked at him like he was crazy."

The riled-up negotiators took a time-out, and when they reconvened Gillman was no longer mentioning his own severance pay or the car leases and instead agreed to kick in $117,000 to meet the workers' final payroll.

By this time, JPMorgan Chase's 40-percent equity in the company had come to light. Gutierrez said he had received an unsolicited call from Bill Daley, JPMorgan Chase's director of social responsibility, offering to come to the table. (The attorney general's office indicated that calls from both their office and Gutierrez summoned Chase to the negotiations.)

Daley is also the brother of Mayor Richard M. Daley, a nemesis-turned-ally of Gutierrez'. Bill Daley was a special counsel on trade issues and later commerce secretary under President Clinton and a member of Obama's transition team—just one more high-profile and powerful supporting actor in the factory occupation drama.

Things were moving forward. The Bank of America officials agreed they would indeed extend a loan to cover the money due the workers. Though it was called a loan, it would be essentially a donation, since there was little hope it would ever be paid back. Bank of America communications staff—who had spent the past few days stunned and confused by suddenly being cast as villains in what had previously been a run-of-the-mill loan issue—shot off a press release touting their offer. It got media attention even with the ongoing Blagojevich story, but it turned out to be a premature misfire since the workers hadn't yet been notified of the deal. The union was adamant about giving the workers the chance to approve any offer. "During the meetings they kept asking us if we would accept different things," said Fried. "They were having trouble understanding we had to bring every decision back to the workers. That's how we operate."

Patricia Robles and the couple's five kids were sitting in their kitchen wrapped in blankets and snacking that night, watching TV for news of the occupation, as they had been almost every minute they weren't actually at the factory. "We would eat and watch, eat some more," remembers Robles. A reporter announced the settlement. The family looked at each other in confusion and dawning giddiness, but Robles knew it couldn't be true, since she knew the workers would have had to approve a settlement and that Armando would have called her. They finally went to bed knowing another day of the occupation was still ahead of them.

WILD WEDNESDAY

Bomb-sniffing dogs and Secret Service agents were stationed in the alley next to the Bank of America building, inspecting the engines of mail trucks heading to the post office across the street and frisking journalists piling into a white minibus. Police cordons lined the sidewalk, and several squad cars were stationed at each end of the block. All this security had nothing to do with the meeting going on inside Bank of America's headquarters, where an increasingly large group of politicians, workers, bankers, and even more lawyers were meeting for the third long day in a row.

Rather, the bank just so happened to be across the street from the federal office building housing President-Elect Obama's transition office, where he would arrive each day after a brisk workout in a friend's apartment building in Hyde Park. Obama was followed the whole way by a busload of journalists and Secret Service vehicles, including one SUV with the back window open to reveal an agent with his machine gun ready, sweeping the horizon for snipers. While immersed in selecting his cabinet and dealing with the fallout from Blagojevich's arrest—reporters were asking if Obama's friend and chief-of-staff-to-be Rahm Emanuel had had any untoward conversations with the governor—Obama had probably pushed the factory occupation out of his mind. But if he happened to look out the window of his office on Wednesday, December 10, he would have gotten a reminder. Nearly 1,000 people were marching in circles around the Bank of America building, with the march passing right in front of the federal building, past the Secret Service, police, and journalists. A plethora of picket signs, hand-painted fabric banners, homemade posters, and flags waved and bounced happily above the throng. There were an abundance of rainbow flags; a gay-rights march protesting the passage of anti-gay-marriage Proposition 8 in California had merged into the Republic rally. Anarchists with bandannas tight over their faces waved black-and-red flags; union members jabbed the air with their respective placards, and affiliates of Interfaith Worker Justice carried signs invoking spirituality and fairness. "They got bailed out, we got sold out!" shouted the crowd. In San Francisco, New York and numerous other cities nationwide, people were also picketing outside Bank of America branches in protests organized by Jobs with Justice. In Little Village, Chicago's heavily Mexican neighborhood where many workers lived, people picketed at a storefront Bank of America branch.

As Robles, Maclin, and the other union reps arrived downtown for the meeting, they could hear the protest chants from three blocks away. The meeting started at 1 p.m. and dragged on for hours. Finally, in the evening, a proposal was put together combining a $1.35 million loan from Bank of America and $400,000 from Chase. "I've never seen a bank lend $1.3 million when they know they won't get it back," marveled Congressman Gutierrez. "And JPMorgan Chase gave the four hundred thousand knowing they'd be second in line to Bank of America as creditors, meaning they would never see the money. But we got them to lend it. It was uncharted territory, it was a wonderful thing."

Finally the offer was brought to the full Republic workforce at the factory. Gutierrez waited outside as the union leaders shared the offer with the other workers and deliberated how to respond. The workers were thrilled to be getting their pay and to have won such a victory. But it wasn't all they had hoped for. Was there still a way to keep the plant open? What about all the work they had put into keeping the company alive for so many years—was that all reduced to 60 days' severance and vacation pay? As part of the agreement, Bank of America had demanded that the company file for Chapter 7 bankruptcy, a process that entails liquidation. This could greatly complicate a bid to keep the place open. All things considered, the workers decided to accept the offer but to continue their fight to keep the plant running. They didn't waste any time: that very night, they christened a new trust fund, "the Window of Opportunity Fund," to raise money to acquire the plant themselves or find a new buyer. But tonight they would accept the banks' offer as a partial victory, and celebrate.

The workers streamed out of plant into the expectant crowd of supporters, pumping their fists and chanting "Yes we can," then segueing into "Yes we did!" "The occupation is over," Robles announced gravely. "We have achieved a victory. We said we would not go out until we got justice. We have it."

"This is about more than just money," added UE regional president Carl Rosen. "It's about what can be achieved when workers organize and stand up for justice. It's also a wake-up call to corporate America that the rules have changed in this country, and there needs to be a greater measure of economic justice for working people."

Back in the factory cafeteria, hidden from the press, the workers, union organizers, and their families began a celebration. A Bank of America official even joined them, with everyone putting the past week's hard feelings and antagonistic statements aside. It was December 10, Gutierrez's fifty-sixth birthday, and the celebration doubled as a birthday party. There were at least three birthday cakes and several cards signed by the workers, he remembers. He took a chocolate cake home and left the other confections for the happy crowd to devour.

Even after decades in activism and politics, Gutierrez felt giddy as he made his way to his oldest daughter's house, balancing the cake precariously as he trod ice-encrusted sidewalks. The next morning, he booked tickets for his delayed holiday trip to Puerto Rico. At the airport, it seemed everyone had heard about the Republic victory. "From the security screeners to the flight attendants and the captain, even all these businessmen—white Anglo-Saxons in suits—everyone was happy for the workers," he says. When he landed in Puerto Rico it seemed a world apart, 50 degrees warmer and lush. But even there, people knew about the workers' victory. There are close ties between the island and Chicago, and many Puerto Ricans had followed the struggle on Chicago's WGN or Spanish-language TV stations. "It was a victory for people there too," the congressman said.

Two months later, Melvin Maclin reminisced about that night, and it sounded like he was still in awe of the situation. "We didn't just negotiate with the company, we went all the way to the corporate headquarters of Bank of America and negotiated with them," he said, a touch of incredulity in his voice:

> A giant like Bank of America—they had to negotiate with us. And they were so happy to see us leave. It was like they wanted to hug us and kiss us and say "Get the fuck out!" Bank of America was never legally obligated to us, but the moment they denied that loan they became morally obligated. They thought we were just a bunch of dumb plant workers. But we showed them we're real living breathing human beings, with rights and families...and power.

U.S. Congressman Luis Gutierrez, left, speaks with Illinois State Treasurer Alexi Giannoulias before meeting with Bank of America executives at the Bank of America building in Chicago. (AP Photo/Paul Beaty)

CHAPTER FIVE

A WINDOW OF OPPORTUNITY

It was Sunday, December 14, four days after their victory, and a group of Republic workers huddled around Robles in a storefront church on 26th Street in Little Village. Under the watchful eyes of an image of the Virgin of Guadalupe, they were making a hasty collective decision of the type they had gained much experience with over the past nine days.

They were in the Amor de Dios church, a social-justice-oriented parish run by the Reverend Jose Landaverde, a colorful and often controversial young minister who had come to the United States from El Salvador after both his parents were killed in the civil war there. Landaverde, a child at the time, had hidden in a latrine to avoid the right-wing death squads.

This afternoon, the church had hosted an impromptu fund-raiser for the Window of Opportunity fund, organized by the immigrants-rights March 10 Coalition. Activists, church members, and immigrant workers laid off from other factories had sat in a circle on a hodge-podge collection of folding chairs and overstuffed couches, listening to the Republic workers describe their struggle and singing along with Latin American protest songs strummed on the guitar by Chilean socialist transplant Orlando Sepulveda. Jorge Mujica, a lithe and passionate journalist-turned-activist with a long gray ponytail, was there in his trademark UE baseball cap. A sad-eyed Mexican woman who had become an activist after her daughter was mysteriously murdered on a U.S. Air Force base in Texas came with her friend, a musician who frequently plays at protests. Activists from the International Socialist Organization who spoke little Spanish but made valiant efforts with the language had trekked from the city's north side for the occasion.

A folding table in the corner held a modest array of soft drinks, chips, and a lone bottle of wine, and young kids chased each other gleefully around the room. Everyone had introduced themselves; several workers who had recently lost their jobs were brimming with indignation and stories they needed to share. It was almost as if the Republic workers had taken on a sacred aura, and just being in their presence made other workers feel they too could fight and win struggles.

"The fight doesn't end with us being paid, this is the start of a movement," declared Robles in Spanish. "The government and banks are allowing our jobs to be sent to China. Here they pay eight dollars an hour, so they send the jobs to Mexico, where they pay eight dollars a day. Then they send the jobs to China, where they pay eight cents an hour. This country is called a superpower, but the way things are going it will end up as a third world-country."

"People are afraid, but it's time to change this fear by fighting, by struggling," added Apolinar Cabrera, taking the floor with his curly-haired young son peeking out shyly but mischievously from behind his legs. "We have to continue."

The crowd included several men who had lost their jobs months ago at the packaging company Olmarc and were promised severance and accrued vacation pay, but never saw the money. The two unions representing them—known in the labor movement as company-aligned—left them high and dry, they said. One older Olmarc worker spoke at such length that organizers had to gently cut him off to allow other people to speak. As the dwindling group polished off the last of the snacks and sodas, Robles called out for Reverend Landaverde, saying the workers had an announcement to make.

"We voted to give the money back to the church," he said, handing a chunky roll of bills totaling $270 worth of small donations to Landaverde. "This church is fighting for undocumented people, fighting for social justice. We've received support from many places we've visited, so we want to give back."

A cheer went up, and some broke into a verse of "Solidarity Forever."

"These are the moments that make your skin tingle!" exclaimed Jorge Mujica.

Landaverde tried to return the money, but Robles wouldn't take it. The gesture was an example of the larger symbolism that the UE workers and the community as a whole had ascribed to their victory and ongoing struggle: it was not only about getting the Republic workers the pay owed them, or even about keeping the factory open. It was all part of a broader fight for workers' rights and empowerment during an economic crisis that has raised the stakes for everyone.

The church itself is an example of these struggles. Landaverde had moved his "mission," as he calls it, into this space 15 days earlier because his former church couldn't handle the crowds drawn by his sermons. Until recently, the space had been occupied by a shoe and clothing store, which, like many small businesses on this commercial strip, went bankrupt in the midst of the recession.

On the block just across the street were five recently vacated storefronts with *For Rent* signs on their windows. Colorful, raucous 26th Street is known as the second-most-lucrative commercial strip in the city of Chicago, after tony Michigan Avenue downtown. It is the heart of the Latino community, so the vacant spaces where taquerias, beauty parlors, dollar stores, and shoe shops used to be symbolized the financial strain that the community was feeling. "The situation is going to get even worse—you see how many businesses have closed just on this block," said Landaverde. "But the Republic workers have given us an example that we can denounce injustice. They have shown us that we can stand up for our rights. When one group of workers triumphs, all workers triumph."

PARTY AT TEAMSTER CITY

This was also the refrain at the official victory celebration two days later, in the cavernous auditorium in Teamster City—the truckers' sprawling union headquarters—on Union Row across the street from the UE building.

Kim Bobo took the podium. A slender, animated woman with fluffy long graying hair and bright eyes, dressed this night in a silky purple blouse, Bobo is executive director of Interfaith Worker Justice. She had just published *Wage Theft in America*, a book detailing how situations like Republic are far from an anomaly.[56] "In the religious community we say Satan is alive and well and takes many forms," Bobo declared fervently. "Sometimes the form is the Republic owners, sometimes it's the Bank of America."

Bobo is an old-fashioned faith-based leader, not afraid to talk about Satan and the battle of good versus evil in hyperbolic and militant terms, and to cast the bosses and the workers in their appropriate roles in the allegory. To Bobo, who has traveled the country meeting with workers toiling in hellish conditions at slaughterhouses and poultry farms, losing fingers and limbs on construction jobs, or even held in virtual slavery picking vegetables, this rhetoric probably doesn't seem so hyperbolic. She led the crowd in a rousing sing-along: "I told Satan to get thee behind, I told Satan to get thee behind. I told Satan to get thee behind" (with an accompanying hand gesture telling Satan to get the hell behind) "Victory today is mine!"

Several hundred religious leaders, top union officials, local politicians, workers from other shuttered factories, and a wide range of activists and community supporters had turned out for the celebration, which featured numerous speeches extolling how the factory occupation had breathed new life into the labor movement and given hope to workers everywhere. It was yet another sign that a bold tactic that might have been frowned upon by politicians and the union establishment in different times is now being embraced with enthusiasm. A staffer said that Congressman Gutierrez's office had been flooded with calls from laid-off workers looking to organize since the occupation. Congresswoman Jan Schakowsky took the stage to declare the Republic workers had made her feel "humbled . . . thrilled . . . and grateful."

"This is one battle in a long struggle to take back our economy and take back our country for working folks," said Fran Tobin of Jobs with Justice, which had organized solidarity rallies nationwide during the occupation.

Chicano troubadour Chuy Negrete circulated among the crowd crooning a song he had composed specially for the Republic workers. Raul Flores, a baby-faced Republic worker, snapped photos with his cell phone, grinning ear to ear. A group of men who had been laid off from a bakery in 2005 with only one day's notice also crowded around Negrete. Interfaith Worker Justice organizers were trying to help them collect money they were still owed as of this writing, but it has been a long struggle. Managers of Heinemann Bakery, a major national chain, had told the workers they would get severance and vacation pay and extended health insurance, but the promises never materialized. Eventually, about 100 workers took a settlement of $1,000 apiece from the company. But a handful are still holding out for their full due—between $16,000 and $22,000, they figure. Gregorio Gonzalez, 48, said they wish they had had the kind of support and organization the Republic workers are enjoying. He laments that they didn't launch a movement at the time they were laid off, and only later teamed up with Interfaith Worker Justice. In the fall of 2008, a judge ruled in their favor, but they still were not paid. With between 15 and 27 years working at Heinemann, none of the men were able to get jobs with as much pay and seniority. One of the workers, 28-year-old Genaro Rodriguez, was hired at another bakery, Gonella, only to have it close down too. He now has no job to support his seven-month-old daughter, whose picture he proudly shows off on his cell phone.

The drumbeat of bad news on the labor and economic fronts had continued in the days immediately after the Republic victory. Pittsburgh-based U.S. Steel had announced the closings of a steel mill in Granite City, Illinois, a Detroit-area site, and an iron ore processing operation in Minnesota, meaning job losses for about 3,500 people. Many of the Granite City workers had gotten their pink slips the same day that Republic closed—December 5. At a Wisconsin fan factory, 164 workers had also just learned they would be laid off.

But this climate seemed to only fuel the feeling of jubilation and determination in Teamster City. The 300-some people rose and joined hands to sing "Solidarity Forever," aided by the lyrics projected on a screen between parallel Christmas trees, American flags, and Teamster emblems.

"History and change has always been about collective action, which is what the UE did last week," said Illinois Labor History Society president Larry Spivak. "The problem we have is most people don't remember our stories. Let's keep telling this story and keep history alive."

Kevin Surace, CEO of Serious Materials. Serious Materials acquired the assets of Republic in February 2009 and plans to rehire 250 union employees tied to spending under the Recovery Act. Surace became interested in Republic after reading news reports of the factory takeover. (Photo courtesy of Serious Materials)

CHAPTER SIX

GETTING SERIOUS

One of the people who heard the Republic story loud and clear was Kevin Surace. He is a socially conscious, technologically savvy San Francisco Bay Area denizen who made out quite well in the dot-com boom and decided to parlay his earnings, along with healthy support from other venture capitalists, into the green economy. He got a slight jump on the market, launching a company called Serious Materials in 2002 before "green" was the hot catchphrase of marketers and consumers everywhere. Serious Materials manufactures energy-efficient residential windows and commercial glass, said to keep in warm or cool air three to four times better than competitors' products. The company also makes ecologically friendly drywall, called Ecorock, using a process that consumes less water and produces less waste than standard drywall. Traditionally, drywall is made out of gypsum, which requires large amounts of heat and hence emits greenhouse gases. Ecorock is made largely from waste diverted from landfills, and it is heated through a chemical reaction rather than fossil-fuel burning, so the company calls it "zero-carbon drywall." They say if it was adopted nationwide, carbon dioxide emissions would be reduced by 25 billion tons. The product has won them significant media attention and awards for green entrepreneurship.

In short, Surace is one of those people who believe you can make money and make the world a better place at the same time. A walking, talking avatar of the youthful businessman who strolls out onto the company's elegantly designed web page says as much. So when Surace read about the Republic workers' plight, he thought he could help out.

During the occupation, the union and their supporters touted Republic's ENERGYSTAR products, describing their windows as "green" investments that should grow in demand with expected national greenhouse-gas reduction mandates and weatherization incentives.[57] In reality, Republic was making high-quality but relatively traditional windows that weren't necessarily market leaders in energy efficiency or green innovation. Surace figured the machinery and workers' expertise could be adapted to make Serious Materials' various energy-efficient window and glass lines. He had been planning to open a Midwestern factory in the future, and with

Republic he could fill this goal while also helping the workers and playing the good guy in a drama unfolding on the national stage.

Surace tracked down Robles' cell phone number and called him to express his interest in buying the company. A few days after Christmas, he flew to Chicago and took a tour of the factory with city councilman Scott Waguespack. (At this point, the factory was empty of workers but still lighted, heated, and guarded around the clock on Bank of America's tab.) Waguespack was encouraged by Surace's interest. The city councilman saw Goose Island and the surrounding banks of the Chicago River as an increasingly forlorn island of industrial holdouts in an otherwise upscale, residential and retail-oriented swath of the city. The sight of the Finkl & Son's fiery forges and massive machinery behind sliding doors flung wide open on summer nights is quite an incongruous sight in the otherwise tony neighborhood. But the city's last working steel mill is slated to be moved to the city's south side, and other nearby industries have also closed. Waguespack thinks light industry and commercial and residential areas should be able to coexist, and he wants to turn his ward into a hub of green technology. He envisions wind turbines and other ecologically friendly technologies being built there. To make this a reality, he plans to lure companies by substantially increasing the internet bandwidth, paying for newcomers' architectural drawings, and offering other tax breaks or subsidies for green manufacturing projects. He's been discussing this in the city council's finance committee and bringing in professors to pick their brains. Surace was just his kind of man.

In early January, Surace officially announced his interest in buying the factory and rehiring all the workers. Union members were excited by the suggestion, and a press release was quickly put out. But the process would not be fast or easy. By this time bankruptcy proceedings were in full swing. A bankruptcy trustee was overseeing meetings of creditors, which is standard practice, going through a painstaking accounting of all the company's assets, debts, and possible future income. Meanwhile, a bankruptcy judge was holding hearings and ready to rule on disputes. The bankruptcy judge would have to okay the sale to Surace, and that would mean Bank of America, the major secured creditor, would also have to agree. Selling the company—or actually, just its physical assets since the company itself no longer existed—might not be the most obviously attractive solution for the bank.[58] The bank's quickest way out of the whole thing would be to liquidate all the assets and recoup as much as possible of the nearly $8 million debt owed them. When asked if Serious Materials' purchase could be profitable for the bank, Surace said, "Profitable? Those days are probably over. But this is likely to be an outstanding opportunity for everyone involved to do the right thing."

ON OTHER FRONTS

On January 6, 2009, the union filed Unfair Labor Practice charges against Republic with the National Labor Relations Board (NLRB), charging that the moving of the equipment, the failure to

give WARN Act notice, and other issues preceding the closing violated their right to collective bargaining. Such charges usually work
their way through the system at a glacial pace, and under President
George W. Bush the NLRB, responsible for overseeing the process,
was considered hostile to workers. As of this writing the Obama
administration has not yet appointed three new NLRB members
to fill vacancies on the five-member board, but labor leaders expect the agency to become more proactive and worker-friendly
under the new administration.[59] (These hopes were bolstered by
Obama's January 2009 appointment of NLRB member Wilma B.
Liebman to the position of NLRB chair: Liebman was originally
appointed by President Clinton and was a frequent opponent of
President Bush.) With the workers paid by the banks' loans and the
company bankrupt, the union was not looking for compensation
or recourse with the NLRB charge. But union leaders figured that,
on principle, they should pursue every avenue to hold Republic
accountable for breaking labor law.

Meanwhile, the city was also asking Republic for its money
back: the nearly $10 million in tax increment financing funds it
had given the company. Various city councilmen and the mayor
himself were demanding that Republic repay the funds, since it
had not fulfilled its promise of keeping jobs. At a January 12 city
council meeting, they ripped into the company. City councilman
Joe Moore, who had previously called for the freeze on Bank of
America business, said, "They accepted city tax dollars on the ba-
sis that they were going to remain in the city of Chicago. To accept

these city tax dollars and do an about-face and run to Iowa to pay workers there less wages and fewer benefits runs contrary to the whole purpose of tax-increment financing."

"Republic clearly knew that something was wrong as their business declined. They didn't tell anybody. They basically just walked out of town on us," added Waguespack. But the city's lawyer said taxpayers are out of luck, because the enforcement period for the TIF is only eight years—and that ended in 2004.[60] Waguespack and Moore didn't want to let the issue drop, and in March, Waguespack introduced an ordinance inspired by Republic demanding more transparency and accountability in the TIF process in general, something that neighborhood groups have been demanding for years. It was another victory to come out of the Republic struggle.

THE BANKRUPTCY CREDITORS MEETING: GILLMAN FEELS THE HEAT

The Republic case became a notorious one within the maze-like confines of Chicago's bankruptcy court, a warren of meeting and hearing rooms on the eighth floor of the Dirksen federal building downtown, just a stone's throw from Bank of America's headquarters. In bankruptcy cases, a bankruptcy judge essentially takes control of a company's or individual's assets and decides how debts will be paid. In most Chapter 7 bankruptcy cases like that of Republic, in which the company is being liquidated, the judge appoints a bankruptcy trustee who oversees most of the process administratively, with the judge hearing any disputes. The trustee holds creditors' meetings where the trustee and creditors ask questions to compile information about the bankrupt party's finances.[61] Administrative staff in Chicago's bankruptcy court knew all about the Republic case, which seemed to have hearings constantly. Bankruptcy trustee Phillip Levey's lead attorney, Scott Clar, got tired of wearing a suit every day because of it.

The facts outlined in the "schedules" filed by Republic with the bankruptcy court were not pretty. In all, Republic owed $32.3 million, not counting "unknown" amounts owed to some creditors and liens on equipment. The debt included $23.7 million in secured debt, meaning debt backed up by assets and first in line to be paid; $1.6 million in unsecured "priority claims"; and almost $7 million in unsecured debt, which is unlikely ever to be paid. The company listed $8.2 million in assets, including equipment, a pending patent, accounts receivable (payments due from other companies, and not necessarily likely to be collected) and even White Sox tickets and 39 pictures (both of unspecified value).[62]

The secured debtors were Bank of America for $7.45 million in loans, Chase for $11.1 million, GE Capital Solutions for $1.2 million, a Pittsburgh window company called VEKA for $3.4 million, a man named Larry Fields for $230,000, and Gillman himself for $320,000; plus several companies with liens on equipment. The unsecured debtors included about half a million dollars owed in state taxes to Illinois; tens of thousands in taxes owed to other state treasuries; $590,000 owed to the Wrigley company, Republic's landlord; and many tens of thousands owed to a slew of companies for metal, lumber, screws, machines, uniforms, delivery, trucking, molding, paper, and other goods and services. Workers with unpaid vacation time were also listed as unsecured creditors, since the schedules apparently had not been revised since the banks paid the workers this money. There was a $300 bill for the window-and-door industry magazine, and even a debt of more than $12,000 to the Bellagio Hotel in Las Vegas, the tab for the "dealers incentive meeting" that Gillman and Dubin attended after securing investment from Chase.[63]

At the first creditors' meeting January 18, Gillman got a grilling. The attorney representing the bankruptcy trustee, Scott Clar, confirmed that Gillman owned about 60 percent of the company, since essentially taking it over by assuming the outstanding debt of about $30 million from his cousin Ron Spielman in 2006. But Gillman stressed that even though he had the majority ownership, once COO Barry Dubin brought in JPMorgan Chase the bank had gotten "super powers, super control" over company decisions. Clar seemed to delight in repeating Gillman's "super powers" phrase, invoking it repeatedly over the lengthy meeting.

When asked why the company closed, Gillman said, "The business could no longer raise capital, it was insolvent. Bank of America pretty much had been squeezing us to get the doors closed." When asked whether the workers had gotten any advance notice of the shutdown, Gillman said there had been discussions in the week or two before the closing. He had been at home at the actual moment the plant closed. (Gillman's listed address is an upscale downtown building that looks like one giant window, many stories of smooth glass panels reflecting the sky and surrounding edifices.) "We were probably not welcome in the facility," said Brian Shaw, the attorney for the company.

Clar walked them painstakingly through the company's tattered finances, ascertaining any outstanding payments that might still be due them, wondering if they'd tried to get back security deposits and what utility bills might still be owed. He seemed constantly annoyed that Gillman appeared unfamiliar with the details of the bankruptcy schedules he himself had signed. Clar repeatedly asked Gillman if he knew what was in the documents and if he had read them. "I have no idea" and "I don't know," Gillman answered frequently, including in regard to the nature of the 39 pictures that adorned the company's walls. Clar asked him about the fate of 11 trailers mentioned as assets in the schedule. Gillman said he assumed they were sitting outside the factory. When the attorney asked pointedly about any trailers that might be in the truckyard on the southwest side of Chicago, "or anywhere else," Gillman deferred, "Not that I know of." Then the attorney pointed out mention in the schedule of machinery at "an Iowa facility," including a frame notch saw, an end mill, a sash welder, a sash corner cleaner, and other saws and tools.

"I don't remember hearing an Iowa facility mentioned . . . does the debtor have an Iowa facility?" asked Clar, seemingly with mock innocence given the publicity around the whole situation. "No it does not," answered Gillman.

Gillman went on to say that the equipment in Iowa was actually owned by GE Capital, and Republic had been trying to buy it from GE. The attorney wanted to hear more. The equipment had been moved in November after Bank of America had told the company to shut down, Gillman said.

"Did Bank of America tell Republic to move the equipment?" Clar asked. "Are you saying that based on Bank of America's request you shut down, you moved the equipment?"

"Well it was clear the facility was shutting down," Gillman said evasively. "At that point the equipment would just be useless."

"You referred to Chase as being in super control—what does that mean?" asked Clar, returning to his pet phrase.

"They ultimately had voting power," said Gillman.

"Alright, was there any vote authorizing the movement of the equipment?"

No.

"So Chase didn't authorize that?"

No.

"Were they asked?"

No.

The equipment moved was worth $92,000, Gillman said, and it was now sitting idle at the manufacturing facility in Red Oak, Iowa, formerly owned by the TRACO company, which Gillman said had about $14 million in revenue. Then the history of Echo Windows, the company that the union thinks was meant to take Republic's business and break the union, came out.

Clar: "Okay, what company operates from that facility now?"

Gillman: "A company called Echo, E-C-H-O."

"When was that formed?"

"It was formed I believe the latter part of November."

"By whom?"

"Well, there were several entities."

"Okay, who are the shareholders?"

"It's a trust held in my wife's name."

"Your wife decided to go in the windows and doors business?"

"Well there's another entity that has an interest…"

"Who are the other directors and officers?"

"None."

"Is Echo Windows and Doors engaged in substantially the same business as Republic?"

"Yes."

Clar went through Republic's four window product lines—Builders, Contour, Allure, and Premier Enhancement Classic—and determined where the equipment that had been used to make each now sat. Gillman said that the equipment used to make the Builders and Contour lines was still at Republic, while the machinery used to make Allure windows was "sitting on trailers on the south side."

"Tell me again why you moved the machinery equipment for the Allure line onto trailers?" pressed the attorney.

"It was clear the business was closing, and there was an attempt to purchase the equipment from GE," responded Gillman.

"Did GE know?"

"We had tried to communicate that with GE…we had been trying to contact GE to notify them of what was going on."

"I understand you were trying to contact them, that's good," said Clar in a deliciously patronizing tone. "But it would be better if you could answer my question. When you moved the equipment onto trailers and to Iowa, did GE know?"

Gillman repeated the same line about trying to notify GE.

"Is there a piece of paper you could show me that shows GE's consent to their equipment being moved to Iowa and south side trailers?"

No document materialized.

In the creditors' meeting, it became increasingly clear that Republic officials had moved GE's equipment to Iowa and to the south side without GE knowing it. The legality of moving the equipment is not clear, but Gillman's own attorney and other attorneys involved with the case say more litigation is likely to ensue. Meanwhile, Clar pushed for more details. He ascertained that seven trailers holding equipment were sitting in the south-side truckyard, in addition to machinery that was sitting idle in Iowa. The equipment had been fastened to the floor at Republic and had had to be unfastened for the moving; the work at least in some cases was done by Republic union members. Gillman said he himself did not authorize or supervise the moving, and he said his wife's company, Echo, paid for it. UE regional president Carl Rosen wanted to know if Echo had reimbursed Republic directly for the workers' labor; Gillman could not say. The bankruptcy attorney circled back to the moving of the equipment again.

"Bank of America, GE Capital, Chase—were any of those entities consulted before you moved the machinery and equipment?" he asked, referring to the secured creditors.

"We already talked about GE," said Gillman.

"And you didn't know if they knew?"

"There were attempts to discuss it with GE in advance."

"Were any of those attempts successful?"

"There might have been some successful attempts, yes," Gillman hemmed.

Clar laughed. "You would be better off just saying you don't know." Then he dropped a bit of a bombshell. "Did you know the value of equipment drops if you move it?" Gillman did not.

Clar switched gears abruptly. He asked about the White Sox season tickets—for good seats, Gillman said—listed among the company's assets. And he pointed out the debt of $320,000 the company owed to Gillman himself, as well as a debt for $60,000 owed to Barry Dubin: the promised bonus he had never received for engineering Chase's investment. He asked about the charge for the Bellagio Hotel. When Gillman described the dealers' incentive retreat that he and Dubin had attended, Clar said, "Why am I not surprised?" And then he asked if the company had paid any debts in the waning days of the business. There were a few notable ones.

Among them: prepayment on car leases for Gillman and Dubin. Gillman's lease was $1,400 a month for a Mercedes. Dubin's lease came to $12,000 total for a Range Rover. Gillman guessed these payments were made in September. Since the company was about to close down, "Did you think that was wise?" Clar asked. Gillman insinuated that he felt justified since the company still owed him $320,000, apparently personal funds he had kicked in previously. "So the way you look at it, this was a way of repaying your debt, right?" Clar asked. "So you were paying yourself back, right? Did you reduce the debt?" Shaw chimed in that if a question might lead to Gillman's direct liability, it should be addressed to his personal attorney.

Eventually Clar opened the floor to other creditors in the room who wanted to question Gillman. Carl Rosen wanted to know what happened to the computers that had been moved out under cover of night. The computers likely contained employees' social security numbers and other personal information, he said. Gillman had no idea where the computers were but told Rosen he had nothing to worry about. They're in a closet somewhere in the suburbs, he eventually offered. "Were all federal laws related to identity theft followed to make sure employees won't be subject to damages?" pressed Rosen. Gillman appeared ready for the meeting to be over. But there were more questions, from the IRS, from the Department of Labor, from a trucking company, from a non-union employee who wanted severance pay. Rosen and Clar were still very interested in who had paid for the shipping of the equipment to Iowa. "Echo!" Gillman said. "How did Echo know what equipment Republic had?" Clar asked, continuing the charade that Echo was a company totally separate and independent from Gillman or Republic.

By the end of the hearing, it was perfectly clear that Echo's creation was inextricably linked with Republic's demise, and those involved had not succeeded in creating any illusions to the contrary.

Republic Owner Richard Gillman at the closing of
the Echo Windows plant in Red Oak, Iowa.
(Photo courtesy of KPTM/FOX 42, Omaha, Nebraska)

CHAPTER SEVEN

ON THE ROAD TO RESISTANCE AND RECOVERY

In the first two weeks of February, usually the most bitterly cold and dreary months in Chicago, a group of Republic workers hit the road for the Resistance and Recovery Tour, a road show taking their story to different down-and-out cities around the Midwest, Northeast, and South. They visited four out of the country's five lowest-median-income cities: Cleveland, Detroit, Buffalo, and Pittsburgh.[64]

They started out in Judson Memorial Church in New York City. Then they hit other northeastern spots, including Hartford, Burlington, Boston, Providence, and Springfield, Massachusetts. Soon they were at one of the UE's flagship sites: Local 506 at the

General Electric locomotive factory in Erie, Pennsylvania, which had won UE recognition in 1940. By early February, the Erie factory had laid off or furloughed hundreds of workers because of downturns in locomotive orders.[65] Most of the layoffs were to be temporary, though they could become permanent. Erie is still feeling the pain of the 2002 shutdown of a century-old International Paper mill that had employed hundreds.[66] Various other Erie factories have closed, including American Meter Co. in 2004, striking at the once-proud industrial identity of the hardscrabble Great Lakes port town. Residents and city officials are currently battling over whether to allow a huge tire incinerator to locate there, a project that promises jobs but that opponents fear will compromise their health and environment.[67] Erie as a whole had lost 2,600 jobs (2 percent of its total) between May 2008 and January 2009, though its economy was actually weathering the storm better than the nation as a whole, thanks in part to the GE factory.[68] UE regional president Andrew Dinkelaker, who had organized the Erie event for the Republic workers, said that unconventional actions like the Republic occupation offer a needed example of resistance. He thinks workers are becoming more militant, and he hopes established union leaderships will back them up. "Even though Republic was a particular situation, it tapped into a groundswell of people being upset about how the economy's being handled and who's benefiting and who's paying," he says. "Workers are at the breaking point where they are willing to take more drastic action. The question becomes, if they take drastic action, are they with an organization that will support them internally?"

When the Republic workers rolled into the Teamsters Hall in Cleveland, they were greeted by a crowd of local workers who had much in common with them. Cleveland had been hurt by factory closings and overall job losses throughout 2008, and more were expected. The state had lost almost 100,000 manufacturing jobs in the past year, and 214,000 jobs in total.[69] But it is a city with a proud blue-collar history and a relatively healthy rate of unionization (14.2 percent, compared to 12.4 percent nationally), so there was much enthusiasm for the UE's strategy and victory.[70] Cleveland is also home to the headquarters of KeyCorp, the financially distressed parent of KeyBank, which received $2.5 billion in TARP bailout money. Cleveland union members had protested at KeyCorp as part of a "corporate campaign" parallel in strategy to the UE's campaign against Bank of America.[71] But in this case, they were opposing KeyCorp's continued financing of Oak Harbor, a Washington trucking company that the Teamsters accuse of provoking and then illegally breaking a strike starting last fall. Cleveland Jobs with Justice coordinator Debbie Kline said that the city's workers had been following the Republic factory occupation since day one. She spoke about it during the organization's program celebrating the United Nations Universal Declaration of Human Rights on December 10. "Their story is just wonderful," said Kline, a veteran of 22 years in social-justice movements. "It's the power of the people—it just shows and proves when people start to organize and come together it can make a difference. It sounds cliché, but it's true." Before their evening event at Cleveland's Teamsters Hall, the Republic workers met with immigrants laboring at a chicken processing plant called Case Farms in Winesburg, Ohio. There, about 130 workers unionized with the UFCW Local 880 who had been on strike since July 2008 were replaced by non-union workers. The poultry industry is notorious for unsafe and grueling working conditions. At Case Farms, workers earned an average $8.10 an hour, $2 to $3 less than at other Ohio poultry plants.[72]

Meanwhile, about 400 people turned out to meet the Republic workers at an IBEW hall in Detroit, long the poster child of shuttered factories and deindustrialization, where an already suffering city has been devastated by the economic crisis and particularly by the auto industry's drastic decline. A city that had already been hemorrhaging jobs and residents has been hard hit by more layoffs and foreclosures in the past year, which sent the median price of a home down to $7,500 in December 2008.[73]

Another of the workers' stops, Pittsburgh, was famously devastated by the collapse of the U.S. steel industry. It has since reinvented itself with tourism, robotics, and other high-tech sectors, but it hasn't escaped the current economic crash. Among other things, Sony is closing the Pittsburgh Technology Center, its last U.S. TV factory, at a cost of 650 jobs.[74] Just a few days after the Republic factory occupation, a similar situation was unfolding at the Commonwealth Medical Center in Aliquippa, not far from Pittsburgh. The medical center began as a non-profit hospital founded by the local steelworkers' union when the mills were booming, but the hospital fell into difficult financial straits, as did the whole region when steel production moved overseas and the local mills closed. But the increasing joblessness and poverty made the hospital's affordable services all the more crucial. In 2007, the hospital was taken over by a for-profit company and renamed the Commonwealth Medical Center. On December 5, 2008 the center filed for bankruptcy protection, and two weeks before Christmas it shut down without giving its workers fair notice and severance pay, continued health benefits... or even their last three weeks of wages. On New Year's Eve, the bankruptcy court overseeing the proceedings decided that executives and "critical employees" (including security guards) of the center could receive $151,000 worth of pay... but nothing for the regular workers, who were represented by the SEIU.[75] The hospital nurses and other workers traveled to Chicago to meet with and protest the center's creditor, Bridge Finance Group, at its headquarters in the Sears Tower. Some Republic workers joined them on a picket line. Then, on Monday, January 26, the hospital workers staged a sit-in at the hospital, as nurses, union reps, and interfaith leaders met with hospital executives inside. When the talks reached a stalemate, police were called to break up the protest. The next day, January 27, the bankruptcy trustee reached an agreement with the union to pay the workers' wages.

Another stop on the Republic workers' road tour, Buffalo, has been struggling economically since steel and heavy industry left the area long before this current crisis, and 2008 brought further blows. In the last two months of 2008, almost 1,000 jobs were lost, including 224 from HSBC bank.[76]

The workers finished their tour in the south. They went to Raleigh, North Carolina, an area that had seen waves of mass layoffs in several industries over the past six months, including healthcare software companies, pharmaceuticals, and electronics. A semiconductor company blaming the slowing economy was moving production to Asia; two software companies cut jobs in a cost-saving merger; and Sony Ericsson was laying off 400 people.[77] Then the workers went to Charleston, West Virginia. With an economy based on coal, the state might have seemed relatively immune to the crisis, since coal remains a linchpin of the country's energy program and didn't seem as vulnerable to economic downturn. But in late January, Patriot Coal Corp. announced 400 layoffs with mines and processing facilities closing, and the move was seen as a harbinger of things to come.[78] The global economic crisis including reduced construction worldwide (coal is burned to make steel as well as electricity) had helped push Appalachian coal to barely over half its price six months ago.

Everywhere the Republic workers went, they found people who were either in the same boat or afraid that they might soon be. Even so, they gave generously to the Republic workers. By the end of the tour, the Window of Opportunity fund had raised $30,000 in contributions. Unions, organizations, and individuals had kicked in everything from pocket change to large checks, showing their gratitude and support for what the UE workers had done and still hoped to do.

BACK TO THE BANKRUPTCY

Carl Rosen and Ron Bender got off the elevator on the eighth floor of the federal building on Friday, February 20, and were greeted with signs directing them to the meeting room for Republic. But when they got there, the lines of chairs were mostly empty. Republic attorney Brian Shaw and Scott Clar, the attorney for the bankruptcy trustee, sat at the front of the room, chatting amiably. A woman representing the Department of Labor sat off to the side. Clar apologized to Rosen that he had not been notified—the meeting had been canceled, since Gillman was not showing up due to some unspecified emergency. Clar, appearing both somewhat miffed and amused, told Rosen that he would issue a motion to compel Gillman to appear at the next creditors' meeting. But they hoped to have important news before then. The bankruptcy judge would hold the next hearing on February 24, at which the fate of the sale to Serious Materials would likely be decided.

The meetings of creditors were a parallel process to the sale and would not affect it. But there were a few wild cards, Clar explained. There were rumors that the owner of the building, the Wrigley gum company, wanted the space for themselves and would not give Serious Materials a lease. In October 2008, Wrigley was bought by candy giant Mars Inc. for $23 billion, in a mutually sweet deal that benefited Wrigley stockholders and allowed Mars to swallow up its competition.

Clar assured Rosen that any talk of Wrigley wanting the building was just rumors. However, Wrigley's board was not scheduled to meet until after the potential sale date. And Bank of America, which had been paying the rent, electricity bills, and 24-hour security costs since the factory occupation, said it would not keep paying after that date.

So Serious Materials could make the purchase without a lease, which might be risky. It could also offer to start paying the costs without making a purchase, to take the burden off Bank of America and buy more time to secure a lease. Serious Materials CEO Kevin Surace had said he would not purchase the company until a collective bargaining agreement was reached with the union, and those negotiations were also still ongoing. But Clar told Rosen, off the record, that the union's prospects looked rosy. "I'm sure they wouldn't risk having your people out there again with signs saying 'Don't let it close down,'" he said with a grin, referring to Bank of America.

Clar explained that as things stood, Bank of America and GE Capital were the only ones who would get anything back from the bankruptcy proceedings; even secured creditor Chase would probably come away empty handed as, the way loans had been crafted, they were behind the other two in line. "It isn't uncommon to see secured lenders take a haircut" he said. But this was more of a buzz cut.

Brian Shaw, Republic's attorney, still seemed shocked by the whole situation. He said it might be precedent-setting. "This could completely change the future of lending, completely! You hear about this happening in other countries, but not in the U.S., at least not in the last few decades." If a public campaign can force a bank to lend—or essentially give, since there was little prospect of being paid back—money to a company, what's to say banks won't consider that a serious risk in deciding whether to lend or not in the future, he asked. "It does change the playing field, it brings the specter of other group activities. Bank of America had the screws turned on them by the public and by the state. It throws another element of risk into lending, all of a sudden there's this public-relations element."

The type of loan that Bank of America gave Republic, backed by collateral, could become much less popular if lenders are afraid that workers could seize the collateral, Shaw thinks.

Worker Ron Bender sat relaxed in his chair as the others wrapped up the now-pointless meeting. Bender had searched for work since the factory closed, but with no luck. "It's hard out there, really hard," he said. "I just hope we can get our jobs back." Like Bender, most of the other workers had looked for work but found little. Some are learning new skills in vocational programs, others are taking English as a Second Language and citizenship classes at community colleges or non-profit organizations. A few have found work, but with far lower wages than they were earning at Republic.

Gillman's own future also looks uncertain. His attorney Warren Lupel said he could not comment for this book because there is litigation, "both pending and impending," meaning both the bankruptcy proceedings and possibly more legal action to come. He also said he wouldn't feel comfortable commenting given that "people are trying to make careers out of this. I can't comment, and he would be a fool to comment," he said of Gillman.

DÉJÀ VU IN IOWA

On Sunday afternoon, February 22, Sandra Schoonover and about 100 other workers at Echo Windows and Doors in Red Oak, Iowa, got a call saying they would not need to come to work the next morning. The factory was closing. After Sharon Gillman had bought the plant about two months earlier, Richard Gillman and two other Republic executives had addressed employees in the Echo break room, painting a cheerful picture of how things would change at the factory. They promised that the product line would increase, people who had been laid off in the past would be rehired, and business would be booming. "They really fired up the employees, he was giving them high hopes and promising them the world," said Ted Schoonover, Sandra's husband and the mayor of the small town. When Republic was closed, the Red Oak workers heard the news and knew about the connection with their new bosses. "We felt bad for them, but you have to take care of yourselves first," noted Schoonover. The scales fell from the Echo employees' eyes soon enough, however. Equipment and materials needed to complete their orders weren't coming in, and they were often sent home early, even when there were orders to be filled, since the materials weren't there. "Everything they said turned out to be empty promises," said Sandra Schoonover. Factory manager Duane Adams, who had worked at the plant for years before the Echo purchase, got an e-mail from Richard Gillman on Saturday, February 21, telling him it was over. "Gillman didn't even have the gall to call himself," said Schoonover. Adams started a phone and e-mail tree over that weekend, spreading the bad news. Human resources manager Mary Lou Friedman was shocked when she got the e-mail about the closing. "It's just devastated this town," she said.

Workers showed up on Monday demanding a meeting with Gillman, whom they had not seen since his pep-rally-like performance when Echo bought the plant. They waited for an hour in the cold, but they caught only a brief glimpse of Gillman as he hurried into a meeting room, where he sat with Adams for nearly four hours. Gillman reportedly agreed to suspend the official closure temporarily while Adams and local officials sought new investors, but the search would be in vain. In a statement, Gillman blamed the closure on bad publicity from the Chicago sit-in, citing "labor strife, continuous labor media stories and accusations" that made customers "nervous."

After the closing notice, more troublesome details about the Echo purchase came to light. One of Gillman's associates, Bill Smith, had formed a limited liability company called Red Oak Real Estate expressly to buy the building and land from TRACO, the previous window and door company. After the plant closed, TRACO had sued Red Oak Real Estate for more than $1 million, saying the company had not been making its mortgage payments or paying utility bills. This meant a risk of the pipes freezing and the building rapidly deteriorating, TRACO's lawyers said.

In Red Oak, industry has waned in recent years as it has across the Midwest. Three years ago, 350 people lost their jobs when the Romech factory that made car seats for Dodge moved to Mexico. The TRACO window and door factory opened 15 years ago and was one of the major employers. There are a few remaining small factories, making goods including corn chips, coffee mugs, hydraulic hoses, and lead batteries, but times are tough all over and there are few new jobs to be had.

"There's really nothing else in the area. You can't go out and get another job," said Schoonover. Most of the employees had been at TRACO for more than a decade, earning somewhere between $10 and $13 an hour, decent wages for a small town. Echo's closure meant the loss of hundreds of thousands of dollars each month in payroll alone, Schoonover said, not to mention the ripple effect on the local economy. Already, a temporary agency that had mainly supplied workers to TRACO/Echo has closed, and residents don't expect the full economic impact to be felt for another few months. Some families had both parents working at the plant; now they have no income or health insurance. And the workers are finding that they may even be responsible for healthcare costs while they were employed, since it turns out the company was not paying its portion of their health insurance premiums, even though insurance payments were being deducted from their wages.[79]

IT'S A DEAL
On Wednesday, February 25, two days after the Iowa plant closed, the Republic workers got the news. The bankruptcy judge had indeed approved the sale to Serious Materials, for $1.45 million. Serious Materials would pay the bankruptcy trustee, who would dole out the money to secured creditors after subtracting costs associated with the bankruptcy process. Serious Materials would be relieved of any future liability to the creditors or for any fines

resulting from the Unfair Labor Practice charges, WARN Act violations or other results of Republic Windows' conduct.[80] A lease
with Wrigley was signed, and the company finalized a collective
bargaining agreement with the union. After a longer and more
complicated process than anyone had expected, things were ready
to fall into place. "There's no question some people, certain banks,
weren't interested" in the sale, Kevin Surace said. "But you had
the union, the city, the mayor's office, an awful lot of people who
wanted to get this done."

The plant would have to be outfitted with much new equipment, Surace noted, a process he expected to take some months.
Then he hoped to ramp up production to hire back any former
workers who wanted to return. As of late April when this book
went to press, about seven Republic workers including Robles
had been rehired to do cleaning and maintenance on the machines. The plant's official reopening was slated for May or June.
Serious Materials managers were determining what Republic
workers still wanted their jobs back and who to hire first. The
union contract guarantees they will all be hired before any new
employees can be considered.

Surace expects to profit significantly from the vaunted stimulus
package, the American Recovery and Reinvestment Act (ARRA),
which provides various subsidies and funds for reducing greenhouse gases. Among other things, it offers $16 billion worth of
incentives for weatherization, which should theoretically fuel the
market for energy-efficient windows and glass.[81] Surace said the
prospect of stimulus dollars was what sealed the deal in his mind.

After the Republic sale was announced, Vice President Joe Biden called it "an excellent example of how the money in the Recovery Act is targeted to spur job creation quickly. These workers will not only earn a paycheck again, they will go back to work creating products that will benefit our long-term future."[82]

As specific details of the stimulus emerged in the weeks following Surace's purchase, things looked even more promising. In March 2009, the Department of Energy released its first installment of $780 million for the weatherization program, which funds government buildings and homeowners to do things like install insulation and efficient windows.[83] Under the ARRA, energy-efficient windows meeting certain specifications and installed through 2010 also qualify for a federal tax credit of up to $1,500. Serious Materials announced that while many windows marketed as energy-efficient would not qualify for the tax credit, most of their windows would.[84]

During a visit to the plant in late April 2009, vice president Joe Biden trumpeted the factory's imminent reopening and the Chicago workers as symbols of hope for the entire nation—and called attention to the factory as an example of the stimulus package at work. "The city of broad shoulders, those shoulders, your shoulders, are built to help ease the burden not only on families here but the burden on families all across this country," said the vice president, joined by workers and politicians in front of a towering display of Serious Materials windows. "One day our children are going to look at the world outside your windows, outside these windows, and see how their future is built on the broad shoulders of folks right here in the city of Chicago."

It turned out that Republic wasn't the only shuttered factory that Serious Materials was saving with the promise of green jobs. On March 16, Serious Materials held a "green ribbon-cutting ceremony" at the former Kensington Windows plant in Vandergrift, Pennsylvania, a struggling former steel town 40 miles east of Pittsburgh. The factory had closed abruptly in October 2008, taking with it 150 jobs.[85] Since the company had filed for bankruptcy, the workers could not collect severance pay. The Kensington sale actually went through before the drawn-out Republic acquisition, and the plant started turning out Serious Materials' energy-efficient windows in January 2009. Between the Pennsylvania plant and Republic, the company plans to increase its production of its SeriousWindows and SeriousGlass product lines tenfold. Pennsylvania Governor Ed Rendell, rehired workers, and the president of the Environmental Defense Fund smiled alongside Surace at the Vandergrift ribbon-cutting as they lauded the potential of green jobs to save the country from economic ruin. "We are going to get serious about efficiency and we are going to bring a new life to American manufacturing," said Surace.[86]

A week later, Serious Materials board member Paul Holland joined President Obama at a White House press briefing on clean energy technology. Obama lauded the company for producing "probably some of the most energy-efficient windows in the world."[87]

THE CREDITORS' MEETING: ROUND THREE

It was St. Patrick's Day in Chicago, and the city was still recovering from a weekend of revelry featuring two drunken, joyous parades and tribes of green-clad people staggering from Irish bar to Irish bar. It was a Tuesday, and after the weekend the decadence was toned down, but there was still a feeling of celebration in the air.

So those cloistered in a bankruptcy meeting room that afternoon were not exactly happy to be there. Republic attorney Brian Shaw looked restless and annoyed right from the start, a feeling that apparently intensified exponentially as the proceedings dragged on for almost three hours. Richard Gillman was there this time. He wore a pale-yellow striped tie, a pinstriped suit, and a tight white shirt. He looked physically uncomfortable but emotionally unflappable, meeting the eyes of the attorneys and those in the audience with a direct, blank stare and a slight smirk on his thick-featured face.

Gillman sat between bankruptcy attorney Scott Clar and Shaw; they seemed determined to get their business done without letting him get away. Two tall, gangly, slightly gaunt, gray-haired men sat on the narrow ends of the long table, facing each other, like bookends to the three-man panel of Clar, Gillman, and Shaw. Bankruptcy trustee Phillip Levey was gentle, almost grandfatherly, speaking in a soft, level voice that belied the strategic and probing nature of his questions. In contrast, Gillman's attorney, Mike Weininger, came off as peeved and testy, rubbing his eyes in exasperation and speaking in staccato outbursts, including telling his client to be quiet.

Carl Rosen, Armando Robles, and Sergio Revuelta sat shoulder to shoulder, halfway back in the rows of mostly unoccupied chairs. Rosen had his typical yellow legal pad and wore a slightly rumpled button-down shirt. Revuelta and Robles wore T-shirts and jeans, Robles a black UE shirt. They occasionally looked wistfully out through the window, where people in shirt sleeves and even shorts meandered across a plaza in the warm air. Just across the plaza and the low roof of the post office they could see the Bank of America headquarters, where the negotiations had been held: the majestic stone columns, the large white Bank of America flag, stained gray from vehicle exhaust, waving in the breeze.

Clar started off the proceedings in the same vein as at the first creditors' meeting exactly two months earlier. He alone seemed to actually be enjoying himself, laughing and smirking often as he took Gillman over familiar territory regarding the pre-paid lease of Gillman's and Dubin's vehicles, the moving of the equipment to Iowa, the unsuccessful attempts to inform GE Capital that its equipment was being moved, and the supposedly coincidental formation of the new window company Echo on December 4, just as Republic was about to close down. Gillman reiterated that he pre-paid the vehicle leases because the company owed him and former COO Barry Dubin money: $320,000 that Gillman himself had sunk into the company and the $60,000 bonus promised to Dubin for securing Chase's investment.

Clar tried to determine whether the cars were officially leased to the company or the men. If it turned out it was the company, he asked if Gillman was prepared to surrender the car to the state. "Absolutely," Gillman said flatly. Gillman didn't know what model Dubin's Range Rover was; his own leased car was a Mercedes S550. The 2009 models, without extras, sell for almost $90,000.

Clar wanted to know where Gillman's old colleague Dubin was and whether he and Gillman were on good terms. Gillman hadn't spoken to Dubin in months and didn't know whether he was still in Chicago. However, Dubin is apparently now spending his days less than a mile from Republic, just northeast of Goose Island at a dog boarding, training, and grooming outfit called Unleashed, where, according to the company's website, he does strategic planning and financial consulting. (Perhaps the simplicity of Unleashed, run by a former high school classmate, appealed to Dubin. Along with Republic, Dubin had previously worked for Arthur Andersen, a Chicago-based international accounting firm that dissolved as a result of its role in the Enron scandal, and Merrill Lynch, now swallowed up by Bank of America.)

Clar pressed about Dubin's $60,000 promised windfall in regard to the Chase deal. "Mr. Dubin was COO, an employee of the company, why would he get a fee?... The Chase transaction would have come under his job description, right?" Clar appeared also suspicious of $27,000 paid to Dubin for negotiating the company's liquidation with Bank of America. "Let's talk bang for the buck here," said Clar. "He got $27,000 for liquidation of the company. Do you think the company got $27,000 worth of services?"

"No, I don't think so," allowed Gillman.

Somehow Clar had obtained an excerpt from an e-mail that Gillman had sent to Dubin in November 2008. "I realize you are frustrated," Gillman had written. "The last thing I want to do is hold you back." The coming week would be crucial to the TRACO deal, the e-mail stressed. "Everyone is nervous... don't give up now Barry, you've come this far."

Clar asked Gillman to again name the four product lines Republic produced, specifying that the equipment for the Allure line was moved onto the trailers bound for Iowa. He asked Gillman if Echo ever sold or marketed the same products as Republic. No, said Gillman.

"Okay, I'm going to show you something that's come into our possession," said Clar with a grin. "A sales brochure... have you ever seen this before?" Gillman wasn't sure, it looked vaguely familiar, he said.

The brochure described Echo Windows as "a convergence of Republic Windows and Doors and TRACO," Clar said triumphantly. "What does that mean?"

Gillman scratched his head, looking nervous and caught off-guard for the first time.

"At one time there was discussion with Bank of America about purchasing the assets," he said vaguely.

"That begs the question, why would you have created a sales document before the company was in business and selling?" said Clar. "Did you create this brochure?"

No.

"Who did?"

The marketing department, Gillman guessed.

"This has hours, an address... one would infer this business was already in existence when this was created," said Clar. "So do you know if this brochure was disseminated to customers?"

"I don't."

"Echo shut down, that's why you weren't here last week?" Clar asked a few moments later. "Everything okay now?" he quipped with mock concern and a healthy laugh. Gillman sat stone-faced.

Clar returned to Gillman's insinuation that Bank of America played some role in the moving of the equipment to Iowa. "Were there discussions with Bank of America where you or anyone specifically advised whether you had or were planning to move the equipment?" he asked.

Gillman sounded like he'd had enough. "I would presume Bank of America really didn't care," he said tersely.

"I didn't ask if they cared, I asked if they knew."

"I believe they knew... I believe it was part of our discussions," Gillman said. "They didn't say, 'Don't move it.'"

"Did they know?"

"There were discussions."

The next hour or so featured Levey and Clar introducing a procession of individuals and limited liability companies (LLCs). They questioned Gillman about his and Republic's relationship to the people and companies, eliciting the refrains "I don't recall" and "I don't know," even in regard to whether Gillman was a member of a given LLC.

Shaw was getting increasingly restless and frustrated, either because of the specific questions or just the seemingly endless proceedings. He tapped his foot, rubbed his eyes, put his head in his hands, fiddled with pieces of plastic and drummed with his pen frenetically. During the previous creditors' meeting, at which Gillman had been a no-show, Shaw had chatted amiably with Clar about their families and a sick dog. Now it looked like he wanted to wring Clar's neck.

It became clear that a number of window-related LLCs, or "entities" as Gillman called them, had been formed by Gillman and his acquaintances, friends, or relatives. Some of these LLCs were customers of Republic and had been getting many thousands of dollars' worth of products from the company without paying their bills.

Gillman's cousin and former Republic owner Ron Spielman was now the president of another large window business called Sound Solutions Windows and Doors, which owed about $209,000 to Republic for orders that Gillman said were probably from 2006.[88] Gillman and his brother Lloyd were both members of the company ABC the Windowguys, which owed a debt of more than $932,000 to Republic, in addition to debts of $3,500 owed by ABC Siding and ABC Supply Co.[89]

Levey was curious about why Republic had allowed its customers to accumulate large unpaid bills when it was so desperate for cash.

"If customers fell outside the terms they would be cut off," Gillman said tersely, describing how he would demand that his brother produce a check from ABC about three times each year. He said the window business is highly seasonal, a pattern that has existed "forever," so racking up large debts in the fall would not be unusual. Levey and Clar did not seem convinced. They also pointed out an outstanding debt of more than $900,000 from Hanson's, a large Michigan-based window and siding company. About two-thirds of it was from the two months before Republic closed.[90]

"Given the fact it was so tight, why didn't you get your regular customers to pay so you could get some cash?" asked Levey.

THE LEGACY LIVES ON:
COLIBRI WORKERS SPREAD THEIR WINGS

The Colibri Group (Colibri means "hummingbird" in the indigenous Taino language of the Caribbean) was formed in 1928 to make mechanical cigarette lighters—a novel invention at the time. The company became a leading manufacturer of high-end lighters, pens, cigar-cutters, cuff links, and other accessories engraved and encrusted with gems. Until recently, its headquarters and two factories in Rhode Island employed a diverse, largely immigrant workforce who spoke at least six languages: English, Spanish, Portuguese, Hmong, Chinese, and Haitian Creole.

But gem-encrusted pens and $100 lighters are the kinds of luxuries most people cut down on during rough times, so it is no surprise that the economic crisis hit Colibri hard. The company suffered several waves of layoffs over the past year. On December 22, 2008, 52-year-old Alda Bonin and a number of other workers were laid off. "Merry Christmas," she told her manager. She didn't mean it sarcastically, but the ill-timed move couldn't be ignored. Bonin is a skilled jewelry mold-maker and kept her own tools at the factory, so she told the manager she needed to collect them. "Don't worry about it," she was told. "The layoff is only temporary, you'll get your job back in early February." Just two years earlier, Bonin had been laid off from another flailing jewelry company, so she was skeptical. She lives about a mile from the factory, and on January 15, when she happened to see her former co-workers walking by in tears, she feared the worst. She quickly got on the phone and learned that her former colleagues had arrived at work to see a sign saying the plant was permanently closed. CEO Jim Fleet had sent an e-mail the previous night, but since many workers didn't have internet connections at home, they had showed up in the morning none the wiser. About 280 workers had lost their jobs, in addition to the previous layoffs.

As at Republic, it seemed Colibri officials had known the company was likely to close. They had desperately sought new investments or a merger over the past year, to no avail. The company had lost $10 million in both 2007 and 2008.[91] But Bonin is furious that they still waited to tell workers until the last minute.

"They started laying off people a little bit at a time," she remembers. "There was hardly anybody in the place. I just wish I was told the truth from the beginning. When they laid off my group, they already knew. So to be told that I was coming back to work, I was deceived."

The Manhattan-based finance company Founders Equity was the majority owner of Colibri. Colibri declared bankruptcy, being $28 million in debt and owing $6 million to vendors.[92] The workers' healthcare was terminated immediately, and their chances of getting new jobs looked very grim. Even before the economic crisis, the state's historic jewelry industry had lost many jobs because of cheaper foreign labor. The crisis meant a severe downturn in demand for jewelry.[93] And other local industries weren't faring much better. The state's unemployment rate for January 2009 was 10.3 percent, higher than the national rate of 7.6 percent that month.[94]

The afternoon of the closing, employee Emilio Blanco, a Dominican immigrant, was at home feeling lost and dejected. He had worked at the company for 22 years, since he was 24 years old. He had done "everything" there, from welding to stone-setting, and he was raising two kids on his income. "I gave them so much, my whole life, and then they just closed the doors on us like we were animals," he said. "I felt like my heart was on the floor."

The workers had no union to turn to, so Blanco called an advice program on a Spanish-language radio station. The DJ gave him the number for Fuerza Laboral (Workers' Power), a grassroots advocacy organization with just two staff members. Director Greg Pearson asked if Blanco could get 10 workers together for a meeting. Twenty-one people showed up, and the Colibri Workers for Rights and Justice was born. On February 3, they drew 250 people to a protest outside the factory, in a snowstorm. On February 6, the Republic workers came through Providence on their Resistance tour, with an event at the Open Table of Christ United Methodist Church. About 50 Colibri workers attended and then met with Robles and Meinster for three hours. The Colibri workers were game for a sit-in or similar direct-action tactic of their own. "It was an amazing moment of solidarity and awareness," said Pearson. "They took the workers through what the process is. Republic had a union, Colibri didn't have any union. Republic got three days' notice, these workers didn't get any notice."

Bonin was highly impressed with Robles and the Republic action. "I thought these people had a lot of strength and confidence in themselves, they were brave and powerful to do this," she said. "When you stick together as a group, you do have more power, you do have more hope."

While many of the Republic workers had experience and training in organizing and direct action thanks to the union and other Chicago campaigns, almost all the Colibri workers were new to the realm. But they dove right in. Since the Colibri factories were already vacated and shuttered, it was too late for an occupation. Instead, they decided to fight through public pressure for their WARN Act pay and accrued vacation time, plus severance pay based on seniority: one extra week for each year of service, a benefit that had been given to workers laid off earlier. Since Colibri was in bankruptcy, as at Republic targeting the company itself would likely not be fruitful. So in a page taken from the Republic playbook, they designed a campaign to pressure Founders Equity and the two banks that were secured creditors: Sovereign Bank and HSBC, a bailout recipient. During a court hearing, former Colibri toolmaker and Vietnam veteran Mike Masi told bank officials, "Banks have insurance. We don't. Banks can wait to be repaid. We can't. For some of us, both wage-earners in the household were working at Colibri and now we are left with zero income. Others of us struggle with health issues and greatly depended on our health insurance, which was cut off as well."[95]

Fuerza Laboral launched a national campaign. Seventy workers rallied at Founders' Manhattan headquarters. They marched on the state capitol. They spearheaded a national letter-writing drive. On March 12, the Rhode Island House of Representatives unanimously passed a resolution supporting the workers and calling for legislation to create a stronger version of the WARN Act on a state level.[96] The city council also passed a resolution of support; the workers brought flowers in thanks. And an attorney working pro bono filed lawsuits regarding WARN Act violations.

On March 19, an auction of Colibri's assets was scheduled. A crowd of about 150 potential buyers was expected, and the auction would be held at Colibri's former headquarters in Providence. The workers figured this was their moment.

They gathered at 9:30 a.m., and police were already lining the street. The workers marched and chanted, waving signs reading RISE TOGETHER, STAY TOGETHER. Teenagers came with musical instruments, and someone said they should dance. Bonin alone started dancing, but felt foolish that no one was joining her, so she grabbed another Colibri worker known as a comedian and the two twirled and dipped as the crowd cheered. Police forced the workers to clear the way when cars drove in for the auction. The first few times the workers complied. Then a group of them sat down in the road and refused to budge. They were quickly arrested. "Seeing the police pulling my friends off the ground, handcuffing them, making them lay down, it was upsetting and emotional at the same time," said Bonin. "But I felt we needed to keep on going for them." Groups of workers sat in the road and got arrested two or three more times over the next few hours.

In all, 14 people were brought to the station and charged with disorderly conduct, including Pearson and about 10 workers. The auction did go on but turnout was low. After the protest, Bonin headed to the station to check on her co-workers. She was relieved to see them coming out three hours later with smiles on their faces.

As Emilio Blanco left the station, his voice was hoarse from all the chanting and cheering, but he was in good spirits. "We're fighting for our rights, we won't stop until we get paid," he said. "This is very important to set an example for other compañeros."

His friend Yannary Sarit, 32, had worked at the company for almost five years and was ready to take their story to Washington, D.C., on the coming weekend for the National People's Action (NPA) conference, an annual convergence of community and activist organizations. This was her first time taking part in activism, but her appetite was whetted. "I thought this was the land of opportunity, but they closed the doors on us," Sarit said. "The American Dream is a myth. We worked so hard for them, and then this. But if we keep fighting, things are going to change."

Bonin was balancing between hope and cynicism about the likelihood of getting their jobs back, but she saw larger meaning in the struggle, regardless of the outcome. By the evening after the protest, she was exhausted and stretched out on the couch watching TV, but her adrenaline was still running. She was looking forward to the next day's strategy meeting and an ongoing fight for justice. Since the layoff she had sent out résumés, but she hadn't heard a word back, not even a note to say her résumé had been received. The jewelry industry will not recover for a long time, she figures. After being laid off twice within a few years, she is ready for a career change. She wants to go back to school to become a medical assistant. The money Colibri owes her would be a big help in launching this dream. "Even if we don't get the money, I feel like I've accomplished something with that group of people," she says. "What we've accomplished already is that another employer won't end up doing what they did to us."

April 27, 2009: Vice President Joe Biden accompanied by U.S. Senators Dick Durbin, left, and Roland Burris along with Chicago mayor Richard M. Daley, center, and Armando Robles, right, visit other workers on an assembly line at Republic, which was recently renamed "Serious Materials Chicago." (AP Photo/M. Spencer Green)

EPILOGUE

In the months following the Republic occupation, it remained in the public consciousness as a symbol of workers' frustration and anger. The mainstream media reported Serious Materials' purchase, the Iowa plant closing, and other updates, and the blogosphere continued to debate the ongoing significance of the occupation. The struggle had clearly resonated even with white-collar professionals who in the past might not have given a second thought to the lives of blue-collar immigrant workers like those at Republic. In response to a *U.S. News and World Report* story, a man laid off from a law firm in October posted:

> Just like Republic Windows they won't pay accrued vacation (I am sitting on over 225 hours) or the WARN Act monies as required by law. You'd think that lawyers would

know what laws to follow and not to break! At least 300 of us have not found new employment in this economy and are looking forward to Crappy Holidays thanks to Heller Ehrman as well as Bank of America and Citibank who are making decisions not to pay us.[97]

The Republic occupation has already inspired at least one major direct action—at Colibri—and scores of individual workers and union organizers across the country say they would consider doing the same thing. Labor experts and union leaders interviewed for this book all say the long-term impact of the Republic struggle and organized labor's prospects in this economic crisis remain to be seen. They point out that the Great Depression was perhaps the most vibrant, militant and innovative era of labor organizing, and they say that if people have the creativity and courage, the current crisis could present similar opportunities.

On blogs and in public comments, financial and business leaders have also said as much. Jerry Roper, president of the Chicagoland Chamber of Commerce, told reporters: "I'd be the first to say to companies that what you saw with workers at Republic Windows will be repeated over and over across the country. We haven't seen this since the thirties."

Labor organizers and academics are in nearly unanimous agreement that the Republic victory would not have been possible even a year earlier: workers would not have been willing to take such risks, the larger public would not have been as sympathetic, and the banks would not have been as vulnerable to pressure.

Despite much media spin portraying the factory occupation as a spontaneous action by workers who just couldn't take it anymore, labor experts and the workers themselves say the occupation was by no means spontaneous, but rather the confluence of painstaking strategy, tireless organization, perfect timing, and a dollop of luck. They say parlaying the Republic victory and future struggles into a larger sea change will take hard work, fearlessness, selflessness, and intelligence on all fronts.

The Republic workers and many Chicago unionists are hopeful that the occupation will inspire a host of similar actions, and they point to situations like Colibri as proof that this is already happening. But academics and journalists who have long covered labor from a sympathetic yet objective perspective are more cynical. Former *Chicago Tribune* reporter and author Steve Franklin, who saw families fall apart and workers take their own lives during the disintegration of the labor movement in the 1980s, doesn't think much has changed. He ponders why American workers don't rise up en masse and take to the streets like their European, Latin American, and Asian counterparts. He attributes the lack of bold action in the United States to a cultural proclivity for individualizing and internalizing one's situation:

American workers didn't take to the streets, they took Pepto-Bismol instead. They blame themselves, they feel like it's their fault, they should have done better, they're embarrassed, they failed. There's an acceptance among American workers that this was their fate and they have to deal with it. There are many reasons blue-collar workers have a hard time showing spine, even though they really have it.

Franklin also points the finger at unions that he says have failed to connect labor struggles to larger issues over past decades. The UE is an exception to this trend, he says, hence their willingness to orchestrate the factory occupation.

The UE members and their supporters say creating public solidarity and pressure is key to revitalizing the labor movement, and, in the modern global economy, perhaps the only way to deal with employers with transient and transnational workforces. A few weeks after Bank of America extended the $1.35 million loan, Pat Holden was adamant that the public and political pressure had nothing to do with the bank's decision. UE organizers find this hard to believe, given that the bank had been dead-set against extending any more credit to the company. Melvin Maclin, Republic attorney Brian Shaw, and others have indicated that bank officials were likely skittish about the precedent-setting possibilities of the struggle. If a group of workers and their supporters could convince a major financial institution to change its policies, even when it was under no legal obligation to do so, would other people want to try the same thing?

Organizers know the public sympathy and support necessary for such a victory can be a fickle thing. Congressman Gutierrez has observed many times in the past how waves of passion and dedication can quickly fade out of the collective consciousness. But so far that has not been the case with Republic.

"I know things like this don't tend to have legs," Gutierrez said, after fielding a call from CNN doing a follow-up on the factory occupation two months after the closing. "But here you had the economy in crisis, the big banks taking our money, and it was Christmas and the workers were out in the cold on the street. Workers are pissed off about the way they're being treated, about the arrogance of corporate America as they are getting hundreds of billions of our dollars. This didn't happen in a vacuum. This was a story demanding a happy ending—people need the underdog to win every now and then. It was a Chicago Christmas Carol."

NOTE ON SOURCES

Quotes, narrative, and scenes are drawn from personal interviews and direct observation except where otherwise indicated. Information and analysis were also drawn from interviews with sources not named in this text, including from Illinois Attorney General Lisa Madigan's office and the U.S. Bankruptcy Court for the Northern District of Illinois. Documents filed with that court were also used.

Republic owner Richard Gillman and his attorneys declined to be interviewed. During and immediately after the factory occupation, multiple calls to Republic's offices and to a former spokesman were not returned. Visits to Gillman's listed residence and a chance encounter with the current resident of his former home also did not yield a meeting. When reached by phone, Gillman's attorney Warren Lupel said neither he nor his client could speak at this point because of possible litigation and because Gillman would be "a fool" to do so. Gillman did not show up at one of the creditor's meetings, where I hoped to meet him in person. At the final creditor's meeting in March, I spoke to him briefly and he confirmed that he would not do an interview "at this time . . . maybe when the time is right." Former Republic COO Barry Dubin could not be reached. An attorney for Republic, Brian Shaw, did talk candidly with me as the company was in bankruptcy proceedings, though he stressed that he did not represent Gillman.

This text was launched as a "live book" on the blog Moby-Lives (mhpbooks.com/mobylives) as the occupation was unfolding and in the following two months. The book was reported and written from the start of the occupation in early December 2008 through mid-April 2009.

ACKNOWLEDGMENTS

First of all, thanks to the workers of UE Local 1110 and the Chicago-based UE staff—in particular Armando Robles, Melvin Maclin, Mark Meinster and Leah Fried—for sharing their stories and insights.

A huge thanks to Kelly Burdick, Dennis Loy Johnson and all of Melville House for hatching the idea for this "live book" and inviting me to take on this exciting and innovative project. I greatly appreciate all their encouragement, speedy hard work, and clear-eyed editing throughout the process. Thanks also to Emily Forman and Ryan Hollon for thinking of me when the idea came up.

And thanks to everyone who lent their perspective and knowledge, including Congressman Luis Gutierrez, Aldermen Ric Muñoz and Scott Waguespack, Bank of America's Pat Holden and

Julie Westermann, Serious Materials CEO Kevin Surace, and many others.

Thanks to all who read the blog and offered their thoughts, with special thanks to labor activist and writer Stephen Edwards. And thanks to professors, journalists, attorneys, and organizers James Wolfinger, Steve Franklin, Curtis Black, Josh Kalven, Jorge Sanchez, Mike Persoon, Jerry Mead-Lucero, Danny Postel, Adam Kader, Jorge Mujica, Martin Unzueta and others, whose analysis and information were invaluable.

Thanks also to *AREA Chicago* and Daniel Tucker for publishing my work on Republic; and to Anka Karewicz, David Schalliol, and Robert Thornton III for their photos.

Thanks to Pat Lydersen, Ken Lydersen, and Jamie Kalven for editing advice on early drafts of the book.

And finally, thanks to Chicago's countless labor and immigrants rights activists who have taught us so much and continued the city's proud history of struggle.

NOTES

1. "Shutdown takes workers by surprise," Colin Perkel. *Sault Star*, July 4, 2008.

2. "East end auto parts employees to resume work today..." Jennifer Lewington. *Globe and Mail*, April 2, 2007. "GM joins severance deal at Collins plant," Tony Van Alphen. *Toronto Star*, April 6, 2007.

3. Statement by Richard Gillman at bankruptcy creditors meeting, Jan. 18, 2009.

4. Slate.com "The Fray" chat room; posting by "Schmutzie," Dec. 8, 2008.

5. *Encyclopedia of Chicago History*, see www.encyclopedia.chicagohistory.org.

6. "Wheels of Industry," Martha Bayne. *The Chicago Reader*, June 29, 2001.

7. "Wrigley hopes new lab will sweeten bottom line," Susan Diesenhouse. *The Chicago Tribune*, Sept. 14, 2005.

8. "Wrigley to shutter last plant in Chicago," John Schmeltzer. *The Chicago Tribune*, June 30, 2005.

9.   *City Council Journal of Proceedings*, pp. 27849–27928: Redevelopment Agreement enacted Sept. 11, 1996.

10. Slate.com "The Fray" chat room; posting by "Schmutzie," Dec. 8, 2008.

11. "Pacesetter windows were once among Omaha's best known products..." Steve Jordon. *Omaha World-Herald*, Sept. 17, 2006.

12. Comment from Richard Gillman, in person, March 19, 2009.

13. Biography at www.unleashedpups.com.

14. Press release issued by Republic Windows and Doors, Feb. 15, 2007.

15. Statements by Richard Gillman in bankruptcy creditors meetings, Jan. 18, 2009 and March 17, 2009.

16. Interview with Pat Holden, Bank of America Midwest government relations manager, and Julie Westermann, Bank of America spokesperson, Jan. 14, 2009.

17. The impact of the economic crisis on the housing industry is evident from, among other indicators, the fact that unemployment of construction workers skyrocketed from 11 percent in January 2008 to 18 percent in January 2009. Manufacturing workers, like those at Republic, suffered doubling unemployment in that period, from 5 to almost 11 percent. Source: *Washington Post*, Feb. 7, 2009.

18. Interview with Bank of America Midwest government relations manager Pat Holden, Jan. 14, 2009.

19. Interview with Bank of America Midwest government relations manager Pat Holden, Jan. 14, 2009.

20. Bankruptcy schedules filed by Republic Windows and Doors list Bank of America as a secured creditor owed $7.45 million. This would presumably include the $1.35 million paid to the Republic workers after the closing.

21. Bank of America website and 2007 Annual Report.

22. Media reports and Bank of America press releases.

23. Bank of America press release.

24. "Troubled Assets Relief Program: Additional Actions Needed to Better Ensure Integrity, Accountability, and Transparency." Gov-

ernment Accountability Office, Dec. 10, 2008. "Troubled Assets Relief Program: Status of Efforts to Address Transparency and Accountability Issues." Government Accountability Office report, Jan. 2009. Media coverage including: "Where's the bank bailout money?" Mary Snow, CNN, Dec. 23, 2008, And "Auditors: We may never know if bank bailout worked," Daniel Wagner. *Huffington Post*, Jan. 30, 2009.

25. "The Deeper Truth about Thain's Ouster from BofA," Bill Saporito. *Time* Magazine. Jan. 25, 2009; and other media reports.

26. "Bank of America plans up to 35,000 job cuts." Associated Press, Dec. 12, 2008, and other media reports.

27. "BofA layoffs are ongoing, but mysterious," Christina Rexrode and Rick Rothacker. *Charlotte Observer*, Feb. 10, 2009.

28. "No pink slips for bailed out bank execs," Matt Apuzzo and Daniel Wagner. Associated Press, Jan. 27, 2009.

29. Interviews with UE organizers.

30. "Feds indict labor leader," Cam Simpson. *Chicago Sun-Times*, Aug. 5, 1999.

31. "Judge faults evidence, clears ex-labor boss on 4 of 11 counts," Matt O'Connor. *Chicago Tribune*, July 10, 2001.

32. Press release from the Assistant United States Attorney, Northern District of Illinois. "Two Chicago Union Officials Indicted on Fraud." Aug. 4, 1999.

33. UE website: www.ranknfile-ue.org/uewho5.html.

34. James Wolfinger, *Philadelphia Divided: Race and Politics in the City of Brotherly Love.* University of North Carolina Press, 2007, p. 138.

35. UE website.

36. Stephen Franklin, *Three Strikes: Labor's Heartland Losses and What They Mean for Working Americans.* Guilford Press, 2002.

37. Stephen Franklin, *Three Strikes: Labor's Heartland Losses and What They Mean for Working Americans.* Guilford Press, 2002.

38. "Workers seek to break from Duff-run union," Andrew Martin and Jorge Luis Mota. *Chicago Tribune*, May 6, 2000.

39. "Azteca foods looks for fresh start…" Kathy Bergen. *Chicago Tribune*, June 1, 2003.

40. Schedules filed in bankruptcy case 08-34113, Dec. 12, 2008, U.S. Bankruptcy Court for the Northern District of Illinois.

41. Stephen Franklin, *Three Strikes: Labor's Heartland Losses and What They Mean for Working Americans.* Guilford Press, 2002.

42. U.S. Department of Labor fact sheet: www.doleta.gov/programs/factsht/warn.htm

43. U.S. Department of Labor fact sheet.

44. "BofA layoffs are ongoing, but mysterious," Christina Rexrode and Rick Rothacker. *The Charlotte Observer*, Feb. 10, 2009.

45. Interview with UE international rep Mark Meinster, Feb. 2009.

46. Republic statement to media, Dec. 10, 2008.

47. Interview with Pat Holden, January 14, 2009.

48. Henry Kraus, *Heroes of Unwritten Story: The UAW, 1934-39.* University of Illinois Press. 1993.

49. Eric Arnesen, *Encyclopedia of U.S. Labor and Working Class History.* CRC Press, 2006, p. 1090.

50. Sources including *The Take*, documentary film by Avi Lewis and Naomi Klein, 2004; and "Here's the chocolate factory, but where has Willy Wonka gone?" by Rory Carroll. *Guardian*, 2007.

51. *American Dream*. Documentary film directed by Barbara Kopple and Cathy Caplan.,1990.

52. Various media reports and firsthand reporting in Immokalee, Fla. and Chicago.

53. Interviews with UE workers, including Armando Robles and Melvin Maclin.

54. "Feds raid pharmacies…" Patrick Ferrell and Chris Fusco. *Chicago Tribune*, Dec. 5, 2008.

55. Interviews with a representative of Illinois Attorney General Lisa Madigan and with UE organizer Mark Meinster.

56. Kim Bobo, *Wage Theft in America.* The New Press, 2009.

57. ENERGYSTAR is a label awarded as part of a joint U.S. Environmental Protection Agency and U.S. Department of Energy program to increase energy efficiency and reduce greenhouse gases.

58. "Secured" means the money owed to the creditor is actually backed up by assets, and they are first in line to be paid with whatever can be squeezed from the liquidated company. When a company closes, employees are usually not secured and are at the end of the line for any due payment

59. Media coverage including "Top NLRB Precedents in Jeopardy Under an Obama Labor Board," Paul Galligan. *New York Law Journal,* Jan. 15, 2009.

60. Interview with Chicago law department spokesperson, Jennifer Hoyle, Jan. 13, 2009; *City Council Journal of Proceedings,* Redevelopment Agreement enacted Sept. 11, 1996, p. 27901.

61. Creditors are those individuals, companies or other parties who are owed debts. U.S. Courts website: Bankruptcy Basics. See www.uscourts.gov/bankruptcy

62. Schedules filed in bankruptcy case 08-34113, Dec. 12, 2008, U.S. Bankruptcy Court for the Northern District of Illinois.

63. Schedules filed in bankruptcy case 08-34113, Dec. 12, 2008, U.S. Bankruptcy Court for the Northern District of Illinois.

64. The U.S. cities with populations of 250,000 or more with the lowest median incomes were Detroit, Cleveland, Miami, Buffalo, Pittsburgh, in that order, according to the American Community Survey Reports of the U.S. Census for 2007. Released August 2008.

65. "GE Cuts 1,550 Jobs," Jim Martin. *The Erie Times-News,* Feb. 11, 2009; and other media reports.

66. "Time runs out for International Paper's Erie, Pa. Mill," Peter Panepento. *Erie Times-News,* May 16, 2002; and other media reports.

67. "Burning Tires for Power," Kari Lydersen. Alternet.org. July 10, 2008.

68. "Erie weathers the recession," Jim Martin, *Erie Times News*. Feb. 8, 2009.

69. "Ohio jobless rate jumps to 8.8 percent…" Gary Pakulski. *The Blade*. Feb. 27, 2009.

70. The 2008 national rate of unionization for wage and salary employees in 2008 was 12.4 percent; however for the private sector it was only 7.6 percent. Source: U.S. Department of Labor's Bureau of Labor Statistics.

71. Cleveland Jobs with Justice website (www.clevelandjwj.org), media reports.

72. "Case Farms Workers to Rally," Lee Morrison. *The Times-Reporter*, Sept. 8, 2008.

73. "Detroit's Outlook Falls Along with Homes Prices," Tim Jones. *The Chicago Tribune*, Jan. 29. 2009.

74. "Sony closing Westmoreland plant," Brad Bumsted. *Pittsburgh Tribune Review*, Dec. 9, 2008.

75. "Judge OK's executive pay at bankrupt Aliquippa hospital," *Pittsburgh Post-Gazette*, Jan. 3, 2009; other media reports.

76. "Recession finally hits the region," David Robinson. *Buffalo News*, Dec. 7, 2008.

77. "Sony Ericsson to lay off 450 RTP Employees," Frank Vinluan. *Triangle Business Journal*, Sept. 8, 2008.

78. "Patriot to Idle W.Va. Mines, Lay off 400." *St. Louis Business Journal*, Jan. 21, 2009.

79. Interview with Ted Schoonover, by phone, February 2009.

80. "Order authorizing the sale of the purchased assets of Republic Windows…:" Filing in U.S. Bankruptcy Court for the Northern District of Illinois Eastern Division. Feb. 24, 2009.

81. ARRAUpdate.com, March 3, 2009.

82. White House press release, March 1, 2009.

83. The Weatherization Assistance Program will allow an average investment of up to $6,500 per home in energy efficiency upgrades and will be available for families making up to 200 percent of the

federal poverty level—about $44,000 a year for a family of four. Source: Environment News Service, March 13, 2009.

84. Serious Materials website.

85. "Serious Materials Re-Opens Former Kensington Windows Plant in Pennsylvania, Initiates Creation of Green Jobs for U.S." *Business Wire*, March 16, 2009.

86. Press release from Serious Materials, Feb. 26, 2009.

87. Media reports, including MIT News Office release, March 23, 2009.

88. Schedules filed in bankruptcy case 08-34113, Dec. 12, 2008, U.S. Bankruptcy Court for the Northern District of Illinois.

89. Schedules filed in bankruptcy case 08-34113, Dec. 12, 2008, U.S. Bankruptcy Court for the Northern District of Illinois.

90. Schedules filed in bankruptcy case 08-34113, Dec. 12, 2008, U.S. Bankruptcy Court for the Northern District of Illinois.

91. "Jewelry Manufacturer Colibri Group Shuts its Doors, Laying off 280," Benjamin Gedan. *The Providence Journal*, Jan. 21, 2009.

92. "Colibri workers protest plant closing," Karen Ziner. *The Providence Journal*, Feb. 3, 2009.

93. "Jewelry Manufacturer Colibri Group Shuts its Doors, Laying off 280," Benjamin Gedan. *The Providence Journal*, Jan. 21, 2009.

94. Rhode Island Department of Labor and Training, U.S. Bureau of Labor Statistics.

95. Fuerza Laboral website, www.fuerza-laboral.org/news.php

96. Press release from the office of Rhode Island State Rep. Roberto DaSilva

97. Comment on *US News & World Report* story, "The Scary Message of Republic & Doors," James Pethokoukis. Comment by Thomas Macentee.